THIS BOOK IS NOT FOR EVERYONE

PLEASE TAKE ONE MINUTE TO REVIEW THE
FOLLOWING PROFILE:

Discipline

- You are an organized person.
- You keep your emotions in check.
- You avoid impulsive decisions.
- You focus on your goals and avoid distractions.
- *You keep at it until it gets done.*

Proactive

- You are self-confident.
- You work to control events before they control you.
- You anticipate obstacles and consider alternative courses of action.
- *You are in charge.*

Investing

- You have established a regular pattern of savings.
- You do not speculate for short term profits.
- Your investment goals are long term in nature.
- You are realistic in your investment expectations.
- You are conservative and seek to understand, measure, and control risk.
- *You are a mature investor working to achieve a financially secure retirement.*

Portfolio Management

- You manage your investments, or are open to the idea of assuming portfolio management.
- You can invest the time necessary to learn and practice a sound investment protocol.
- You are comfortable with the basic math required to evaluate securities.

Continued (over) ⊃

- You have a basic knowledge of investing and finance, but:

    You have limited knowledge of the types and characteristics of investment options;

    You have no structured system to determine portfolio composition.

- *You are on the right path but not sure of the final steps necessary to reach your goals.*

IS THIS YOUR PROFILE?

If not, then this book will not be of interest to you.

<u>If so, this book will help you build a safe, steady, secure income portfolio.</u>

The Organic Dividend Portfolio

Grow and Harvest Dividends
for a Secure and Peaceful Future

Steve Bennett, M.B.A.

THE ORGANIC DIVIDEND PORTFOLIO
© 2016 by Steve Bennett, M.B.A.

All rights reserved

Book and cover design by Jo-Anne Rosen of Wordrunner Press

Cover photograph by Lisa Lombardi Raines

Wordrunner Press
Petaluma, California

"The best way to predict the future is to create it."

— *Peter Drucker, Management Author and Educator*

"I think that retirees are well advised to try to have portfolios that generate as much of their income organically as possible, consistent with their comfort levels.

This is why I write so much about dividend growth investing, because the ultimate goal of that strategy is to have all of your income generated organically, including the annual increases to cover inflation.

If you reach that stage, it guarantees that your portfolio's success rate will be 100%. And if it is important to you, it also practically guarantees an inheritance to pass on to your heirs."

— David Van Knapp, Seeking Alpha.com contributor
May 1, 2015

OK, another book on investing.

Why should I buy this one?

What's new? What's different?

Hello!

My name is Steve Bennett.

I am a Dividend Growth Investor.

I would like to tell you what this investment strategy entails and what it can accomplish.

In order to do that, here is what I intend to do – and what I *do not* intend to do – in this book.

I will not waste your time with motivational gibberish.

There will be no cheerleading about:

- The importance of saving, setting goals, having a budget, and other sixth grade stuff.
- Examining your "emotional profile," "personal risk tolerance," or "investment style"

If you don't know who you are, I'm sure not about to try and tell you!

I will do my very best to avoid boring you to death,

as most investment books do.

- I will avoid mind-numbing, insignificant detail and the T.M.I. (Too Much Information) syndrome
- I will stay on point, remain focused, and avoid digression
- I will edit the content carefully
- I will only repeat myself when I think that a key point needs to be strongly emphasized
- I offer a straightforward text of the Why/What/How/When of Dividend Growth Investing

Above all, I will make this book as practical and "actionable" as possible.

Virtually every investment book I have ever read falls down when it comes to the most important matter at hand: *Analyzing a stock for purchase.* The reader is presented with dozens of items/metrics "to consider." These include a myriad of financial ratios, growth rates, performance and volatility data, industry comparables, competitive strengths, credit ratings, tax considerations, and so forth.

T.M.I. !

What are you supposed to do with all these "considerations"?

The reader has no guidance to determine which metrics are the most important, and the reader has no unified model to convert these metrics into a ranking system for purchase.

This book is different.

- I focus on a ten specific metrics that I believe are the most important in evaluating a company's character and strengths. I will define these metrics clearly and weight them by importance.
- I have created a straightforward model that will evaluate the weighted metrics for each company under review. The model will produce a final ranking score for each company that can be compared apples-to-apples with other companies to determine which are best to buy.
- In this way the reader will have a rigorous, quantitative protocol in place so that all potential security acquisitions will be subjected to the same strict standards and requirements. This discipline will greatly reduce the emotional, subjective, and impulsive behavior that can ruin the creation of a coherent, consistent portfolio.

I want you to take over the management of your portfolio. Forget the "experts"!

YOU CAN DO THIS !

Author's Note

I grew up on Long Island and I am a proud graduate of the Manhasset High School class of 1962. I went to Swarthmore College and received a B.A. degree in Economics is 1966. I then headed west and studied at the University of California, receiving an M.B.A degree in Finance in March of 1968.

I began a career in banking in Philadelphia later that spring, and remained in banking in the Philadelphia area for 25 years. I started out in operations but moved into commercial lending after two years. I spent the remainder of my banking career lending money to small and medium-size private companies located throughout the Delaware Valley.

My wife Georgia started her own company in 1991 and I decided that that looked like a pretty good idea, and in 1993 I founded Funding Resources, a financing consulting firm that helped businesses negotiate and obtain credit support from banks, commercial finance companies, and private lenders.

My daughter Tina is a literary agent with William Morris Entertainment in New York City, and my daughter Lisa is a psychologist in Reston Virginia. Georgia's son Charlie is a multi-talented artist living in Chicago. We have four wonderful grandchildren, who will ultimately have to resolve how they can all become President of the United States.

Georgia and I retired to Maine in 2009. We love our new home, as do our Jack Russell Terrorists, Elva and Sophie.

Disclaimer of Warranty

This is a book about investing. Investing involves risk. It is totally impossible to eliminate this risk.

I really feel kind of silly having to say that, because I can't believe that anyone interested in reading this book – or for that matter anyone who can read *period* – needs to be lectured about investment risk. But I guess there could always be some overzealous investor who might try to sue me because he didn't make a killing after reading this book. So regretfully I will have to take up some space with the following:

WHILE THE AUTHOR HAS USED HIS BEST EFFORTS TO PROVIDE CONTENT THAT IS ACCURATE, THE AUTHOR MAKES NO REPRESENTATIONS OR WARRANTIES WITH RESPECT TO THE ACCURACY OR COMPLETENESS OF THE CONTENT OF THIS BOOK AND SPECIFICALLY DISCLAIMS ANY IMPLIED OR PERCEIVED WARRANTIES OF FITNESS FOR A PARTICULAR PURPOSE. THE STRATEGIES CONTAINED HEREIN MAY NOT BE SUITABLE FOR EVERY SITUATION.

THE AUTHOR IS NOT ENGAGED, AND HAS NEVER BEEN ENGAGED, IN THE INVESTMENT INDUSTRY AND IS NOT A LICENSED, CERTIFIED, OR REGISTERED INVESTMENT PROFESSIONAL.

THERE IS NO WARRANTY OFFFERED OR IMPLIED THAT THE TEXT, EXAMPLES, OR STRATEGIES OFFERED IN THIS BOOK WILL PRODUCE SATISFACTORY OR PROFITABE INVESTMENT RESULTS.

THE AUTHOR SPECIFICALLY REQUESTS THAT THE READER DISCUSS THE STRATEGIES PRESENTED IN THIS BOOK WITH A LICENSED INVESTMENT PROFESSIONAL BEFORE UNDERTAKING ANY ACTION BASED UPON SUCH STRATEGIES.

Financial Calculator

This book will establish a quantitative model to measure, evaluate, and compare securities. This will require certain mathematical calculations. Among the calculations that are included in my model are:

Five year Weighted Average / Dividend growth
Five year Weighted Average / Operating Cash Flow growth
Three year Weighted Average / Dividend coverage
Weighted Average of Total Returns for 3, 5, and 10 years
Ten year Standard Deviation / Total Returns

These terms are all defined in the attachments that follow at the end of the book, and examples of the calculations are given. However, for those readers who are not particularly interested in making these calculations by hand, I have developed an Excel spreadsheet that will perform these calculations.

I would be happy to Email this spreadsheet to anyone who would like to use it.

My Email address is: shustonbennett@gmail.com

I would also welcome any questions or comments you may have after reading this book.

Best Regards,
Steve Bennett

Contents

The Organic
Dividend Portfolio

Introduction

In 2009 my wife Georgia and I moved to Maine from Pennsylvania as we approached the end of our working careers. As with any permanent, long distance move, we had to develop an entirely new roster of professionals: doctors, dentists, lawyers, insurance agents, building contractors, auto mechanics, and so forth. And of course we needed to find a new investment advisor, after the disaster of 2008.

Over the 27 years that we have been married, Georgia and I have relied on the services of several investment advisory firms to manage our money. We have been with large banks, small banks, regional brokerage firms, national investment companies, and individual practitioners. I am sorry to say that in almost every case we have been disappointed. Poor performance, miscommunication, hidden fees, unresponsive customer service: You name it – we've been there.

The company we ultimately selected in the spring of 2009 underperformed the market that year, a year of significant recovery. Results in 2010 were also below market averages. In 2011, the S&P 500 stock average was dead flat, opening and closing the year at 1257. Including dividends, the S&P Total Return Index in 2011 was up 2.1%. Yet the value of our portfolio declined over 4%.

In reviewing the 2011 performance, I mentioned to Georgia – with some sour amusement – that we had in effect paid our advisor a fee of 1½% to lose the other 2½%!

Dead silence.

Very slowly, Georgia said: "Say that again."

Knowing my wife as I do, and sensing a very keen change in the tenor of her voice, I cautiously repeated my comment. And again, dead silence. And then she said:

"Do you actually mean to tell me that we paid this guy (x) thousand dollars to lose almost twice that amount??!!?!"

That was the instant that I knew things had to change. There had to be a better way!

It was no longer a matter of finding yet another advisor – we had gone down that road once too often.

No one else would provide the care and competence we were looking for – and had a right to expect.

I was going to have to learn to do this myself.

Over the past four years I have undertaken a new "job": Teaching myself everything I could find out and assimilate about investing. I have learned a great deal, not only about the subject itself, but also about the fixed perceptions and attitudes – ingrained in me over the past 40 years – that restricted my thinking and whole approach to investing and portfolio management. I have ultimately abandoned these old perceptions and replaced them with a new and very simple strategy:

Dividend Growth Investing

I look forward to explaining this strategy to you. I sincerely believe that it will empower you to reach the level of financial strength and safety that we all seek. Best of luck!

Steve Bennett

What Is an Organic Portfolio?

During the past decade, many Americans have at last come to understand that "you are what you eat." We as a nation are beginning to focus seriously on the composition and construction of a healthy diet. So when we hear the word "organic" – and we hear it every day – we normally associate it in a very positive way with the growing, processing, and preparation of what we eat. If a food is organic, then it is "pure" in the sense that man hasn't messed with it too much.

But "organic" is actually a pretty versatile adjective, with a variety of meanings well beyond the food industry. Among its other definitions, "organic" describes something that is derived from a living organism. That is the most basic definition. "Organic" also describes something that is simple, basic, and close to nature. Finally, "organic" refers to something *fundamental, structural, and constitutional*.

What I am going to write about in this book is an approach to investing that combines all of the above definitions – all of the qualities – of the word "organic." This adjective appeals to me as a very sensible way to think about an investment portfolio – as a living organism like a garden, orchard or vineyard that continuously produces something that is essential to our health, happiness, and comfort. If we create this organism with the confidence of a clear vision, tend to it carefully, stay the course with discipline and commitment, avoid harmful distractions, and fertilize with the very product that the organism itself creates, then we should enjoy the bounty of healthy, growing harvests for years to come.

To be specific, here are the "organic" qualities that I want to establish in an investment portfolio:

FUNDAMENTAL

- The portfolio must be constructed to achieve the fundamental goal of investing: *Income*

If you were asked to define the core objective of investing, how would you answer? Would you say "To Get Rich"? Or "To Beat The Market"? How about "Buy Low Sell High"? These are phrases that we hear frequently, but they all miss the mark because they do not chart out a precise course of action.

I define the fundamental goal of investing as follows:

To provide an adequate and consistent stream of income to support our lifestyle after other sources of income have declined or ceased.

So the most basic characteristic of my portfolio is a focus on income creation. Please note that this is a *very different goal than the pursuit of capital gains.*

RELIABLE

- We expect that income creation will occur in a predictable and dependable fashion with only modest involvement or additional action on our part.

We expect that an orchard or vineyard will continue to produce year after year in a reliable fashion.

Of course we will need to tend to it, fertilize it, and protect it from harmful pests or diseases. But if we do these things, we expect the organism itself to do the "heavy lifting": producing consistently over the years. We rely on the organism – the portfolio itself – to do the work of creating income without constant interference, adjustment, or action on our part.

HEALTHY

- We will seek out and purchase only the strongest, healthiest, and most seasoned companies.

If we were to start a vineyard, we would look for the very best soil, the ideal climate, and the sturdiest vines so that we would maximize our chances for optimum income generation. So too with our investment portfolio. To produce reliable, consistent income, we will focus on companies that have demonstrated consistent, growing cash returns to shareholders over an extended period. These will be quality companies with strong balance sheets, substantial competitive strength, seasoned management, and consistent cash flow. We will be investing for the long term and we expect that these companies will continue to weather the test of time.

SIMPLE

- We will devise a simple protocol to establish discipline in evaluating and buying securities.

Natural products are simple products. Good seed, good soil, some sun, some rain, organic fertilizer, and you should be good to go. Creating a portfolio should also be a simple process, in which a group of metrics – ten in total – are measured and weighted to produce a straightforward ranking system. We will follow certain basic qualitative and quantitative steps to establish a disciplined selection process.

AUTONOMOUS

- We will control the portfolio ourselves with little or no outside involvement.

Growers of organic food seek to eliminate the processors, wholesalers, and retailers in the food industry and sell directly to consumers in what has become known as "farm to table" delivery. Both growers and consumers benefit from such an arrangement where is it practical, as the food itself is fresher and middlemen expenses have been eliminated. In a similar fashion, once we have mastered the basic protocol we will be able to invest on our own without the involvement of brokers, bankers, or advisors.

We will eliminate advisor fees and we will be in control.

GROWING

- We will create an income stream that will experience geometric growth.

We expect that, once planted with care, a garden, orchard, or vineyard will grow, and ideally this growth will occur through the normal forces of nature with little involvement from human agency. And this is *exactly* what we will expect from our organic portfolio. We will see how three basic forces – dividend growth, dividend reinvestment, and compound interest – will combine to produce an accelerated level of wealth creation with very little work on our part after purchase.

In order to construct an organic portfolio, we will need to change the way we think about and approach investing.

We will move away from an approach to wealth creation based on increasing share value.
This requires that we or our advisors do the work and succeed in buying low and selling high.

We will adopt an approach to wealth creation based on growing cash dividends and distributions.
This requires that the corporations we own do the work without our continuous involvement.
So our money will work for us Instead of we working for our money!

What Is a 100% Organic Portfolio?

Throughout this book I will make reference to a portfolio that is "100% Organic."

What do I mean by this phrase?

The answer is straightforward. A 100% organic portfolio throws off enough income so that, when added to other sources of retirement income such as social security, annuities, and pensions:

- The Investor receives enough income to cover all his normal living expenses and pay his taxes.
- Portfolio income grows enough to at least cover inflation.

This is the ultimate goal – the pinnacle – of investing. If you can reach this state, then you will never *have* to sell a single share of stock. Of course you may decide that you *want* to sell stock for any number of special reasons, but you are in a perfect defensive position. As long as you stay on budget, or unless inflation gets out of control, then:

You will be in firm control of your financial affairs.
Your income will no longer be affected by market price fluctuations.

In fact, as we will show later, as you build your portfolio you may actually benefit from market price corrections since you will be able to buy more shares at lower prices, providing additional dividend income to compound wealth accumulation.

If you follow the approach that we advocate in this book – Dividend Growth Investing – you will put powerful mathematic principals into action that will help you move closer to this goal. Whether you get to a 100% organic position will depend on a host of personal, professional, health, lifestyle, age, and financial circumstances, but if you pursue DGI with discipline and focus, you will:

- Develop a higher level of *control* over your income;
- Develop a more *consistent* stream of income;
- Enjoy the *comfort* of a Sleep-Well-At-Night (SWAN) portfolio.

And even if you do not achieve a 100% organic portfolio – which means you will periodically have to sell some assets to pay the bills – you are still better off if you follow the DGI approach. For every dollar of income that your portfolio generates, that is one dollar less of stock that you have to sell.

Good Reading and Good Luck!

SECTION ONE

WHY

"Watching your stock portfolio go up in smoke twice in one decade is not a pleasant experience. What got me through it without making the huge mistake of selling any of my stocks?

"Dividends."

— *Buyandhold2012, Seeking Alpha contributor*
seekingalpha.com, June 27, 2015

What This Section Will Cover

When studying the history of stock market activity in the United States, it appears clear that stock market returns tend to "revert to the mean" over long periods of time. What this means in specific terms is that given enough time – 50 years or more – the inflation-adjusted real return of the stock market will fall in a very tight range around 6.5%. This fact has been measured over a number of periods of long duration dating all the way back to the very early days of the nineteenth century.

However, the stability of returns in the long run in no way implies stability in the short run. The market can go for a decade or longer producing returns that can be substantially above or substantially below the long-term average.

In the real world, most investment portfolios are built slowly over time. Gradually increasing contributions, combined with principal compounding, create a geometric growth pattern for portfolio construction in which the last few years of growth can become absolutely crucial to a successful conclusion. If this latter investing period – wherein the portfolio has reached "critical mass" – should occur during a prolonged or sharp market break, the investor may simply not have enough time or remaining capital to recover.

Just as a market downturn can harm a portfolio *in the making*, the same damage can occur to a portfolio *already made*. Investors who retired at the end of the last century saw their portfolios crushed by the dot.com collapse of 2000-2002, and crushed again by the financial chaos of 2008.

These investors were harmed because:

- They relied on market appreciation – capital gains – to fund their retirement.
- They were victimized by market forces utterly beyond their control.

This book proposes an alternative approach to investing. This is not a radical new approach, but rather a very simple one that *emphasizes stock yield – income – over stock price.* By investing in strong, established companies that pay increasing dividends year after year, an investor can harness the power of dividend growth, compounded over time, to produce predictable, stable funding for retirement.

The investor will:

- Take control of his financial future
- Achieve consistent returns
- Experience relief from the uncertainty of random market events

> *This book proposes an investment strategy*
> *in which the investor succeeds*
> *when he buys a stock*
> *rather than when he sells it*

My Thirty-Year Lesson

I began investing in 1981. I was a banker then, and the Prime Rate had just hit 21%. The first security I ever bought was a 10-year US Treasury Zero Coupon Bond with a yield to maturity of 15.75%.

It was – and still remains – the highest rate ever paid on any 10-year US government obligation.

So here was a totally risk-free investment – paying an extraordinary rate of interest – that is absolutely unavailable today on any type of investment, save those of the very highest leverage and risk.

What a great time to be an investor!

One year later, the great bull market of 1982 began. And what a ride *that* was! Over a 17½ year period that stretched from June 1982 to December 1999, the Dow Jones Industrial Average rose from 777 to 11,497. That's an increase of 1380%, which is so large as to be meaningless.

But put another way, that represented a *compound annual growth rate of 16.6%*.

Every year, year after year, for seventeen and one-half years.

The value of your investments grew 16.6%.

So if you invested $100,000 in June 1982, that sum would have grown to $1,469,686 by December 1999.

As I said, what a great time to be an investor![1]

So from my late 30's, through my 40's, and well into my 50's – my primary investing years – it was win/win for investors. The stock market did hit some bumps of course – it always does – but quickly recovered and went on to new heights. And even

1 There is a story that Albert Einstein was once asked to name the most powerful force in the universe. According to the story, he responded without hesitation: "Compound Interest"

if you avoided the stock market, you could earn 5% or more on a riskless bank CD or Treasury security. Talk about low hanging fruit!

And if anyone had tried to talk to me then about the importance of dividends and the role they play in my total return, I would have dismissed them out of hand. Dividends Shmividends! Who cares! Just frosting on the ever-growing cake of capital gains.

Ah, but what happened next? Remember the Dow Jones Average of 11,497, which is where the market stood on January 1, 2000. Let's move forward nearly twelve years to November 28, 2011. Where was the market that day, *well over a decade later?*

11,497!
NO GAIN!

Some History

For the near-30 year period that I have discussed above (June 1982 to December 2011), the compound annual growth rate of the Dow Jones Industrial Average was 9.56%. This number is reasonably close to the "conventional" nominal market growth rate of 8-9%.[2]

However, this "nice" average growth rate is *completely lopsided*. The rate dissolves into two very different periods: The first period of 17½ years produced a growth rate of 16.6%, while the last period of 12 years produced a rate of 0.00%. Quite a difference!

Those of us who grew up investing in the 80's and 90's came to *believe that capital gains were predictable and substantial.* We learned a very different lesson after the dot-com collapse in 2000 and the broader financial melt-down in 2008. And we are *still learning that lesson.*

What is of significant interest here is that the results of this particular thirty year period are quite similar to the growth rates observed over other lengthy periods in US stock market history. If one studies various periods of long duration, a similar pattern emerges. Looking at the *entirety* of each such period, the market tends to "revert to the mean" and produces nominal returns between 7-10% and real returns (inflation adjusted) around 6.5%.

In fact, the long term stability of real returns – ranging closely around 6.5% – has persisted in the US stock market over various major time periods *for over 200 years.*

---

2   The nominal growth rate is calculated based on absolute dollar amounts without adjusting for inflation. The real growth rate is adjusted for inflation, and is more significant for long term investors.

Period	Length	Nominal Return	Inflation	Real Return
1802-2012	210 Years	8.1%	1.4%	6.6%
1871-2012	141 Years	8.7%	2.0%	6.5%
1802-1870	68 Years	6.9%	0.1%	6.7%
1871-1925	54 Years	7.3%	0.6%	6.6%
1926-2012	86 Years	9.6%	3.0%	6.4%
1946-2012	66 Years	10.5%	3.9%	6.4%

Source: Jeremy Siegel, *Stocks for the Long Run*, McGraw Hill, 2014, p. 83

As professor Jeremy Siegel notes:

"The long-term stability of stock returns has persisted despite the dramatic changes that have taken place in our society during the last two centuries. The United States evolved from an agricultural to an industrial economy and then to the postindustrial, service- and technology-oriented economy it is today. The world shifted from a gold-based standard to a paper money standard. And information, which once took weeks to cross the country, can now be instantaneously transmitted and simultaneously broadcast around the world. Yet despite mammoth changes in the basic factors generating wealth for shareholders, equity returns have shown an astounding stability."[3]

Historic evidence strongly supports the conclusion that – *given enough time* – investments in US equities will perform in a tight and predictable manner and return a real yield very close to 6.5%. As professor Siegel points out, this really is a remarkable – almost counterintuitive – conclusion. This country has experienced several major wars, financial panics, prolonged droughts, speculative outbursts, recessions, depressions, and extraordinary economic, financial, demographic, and technological evolution, and yet the stock market marches on to a very steady cadence.

---

3   Jeremy Siegel, *Stocks for the Long Run*, McGraw Hill, 2014, pp. 81-84.

However – and this is the key point I want to make in this book – stability in the long run in no way guarantees stability in the short run.[4]

Consider the following periods:

Period	Length	Nominal Return	Inflation	Real Return
1946 – 1965	19 Years	13.1%	2.8%	10.0%
1966 – 1981	15 Years	6.6%	7.0%	-0.4%
1982 – 1999	17 Years	17.3%	3.3%	13.6%
2000 – 2012	12 Years	2.7%	2.4%	0.3%

Source: Jeremy Siegel, Stocks for the Long Run, McGraw Hill, 2014, p.83

Look at the differences here! During my primary investment period, seventeen years from 1982 -1999, nominal returns were exceptional and inflation was modest. The result: real returns were 13.6%, the best of any post-war period studied above. But now look at the preceding period of fifteen years, from 1966 – 1981. Nominal returns were modest and inflation – rampant in the 1970s – was severe. The result: real returns were a *negative 0.4%. Your stocks lost real value* – their purchasing power – over this extended fifteen year period of time.

So here is the fundamental quandary of stock investing. Stocks seem steady and predictable over the (very) long run, but performance can be widely and wildly inconsistent over shorter periods of time. So the answer seems to be that one should invest over the longest time frame possible.

But is that practical advice – in the real world? For the average saver or typical investor?

Even for the most disciplined and proactive investor?

Consider a very special situation. A person inherits $100,000 on his or her 21st birthday and invests in a diversified portfolio of stocks. This person does not need to live on these funds and

---

4   Ibid.

plans to use them to fund a charitable trust upon his death. So if the individual lives to be 80, the investment period is 60 years and the anticipation of a 6.5% real yield is reasonable. The funds at death would total $4,375,000.

But this is not a realistic scenario for 99.9% of the saving/ investing public. In the real world, we begin saving modest amounts as young adults and increase our savings over time. So while we may indeed save and invest over a 40-50 year period, *we are not true long-term investors*.

The reason is simple: *We do not have the full amount invested for the full period*. This is the only condition under which we can claim to be true long-term investors for that particular period of time.

If we are gradually increasing the investment amount, the *effective* investment period will always be less, and in most cases considerably less, that the full period.

Building an Investment Portfolio in the Real World

One way to think about building a real portfolio is to *consider the halfway point in value creation.*

Let me give you an example of what this means.

Presume that an individual invests $5,000 in a stock portfolio every year for 10 years at a compound rate of 6.5%. The "value creation" of this portfolio looks like this:

END OF	Contribution	Accumulated Contributions	Total Value
Year 1	$5,000	$ 5,000	$ 5,325
Year 2	5,000	10,000	10,996
Year 3	5,000	15,000	17,035
Year 4	5,000	20,000	23,467
Year 5	5,000	25,000	30,317
Year 6	5,000	30,000	37,612
Year 7	5,000	35,000	45,381
Year 8	5,000	40,000	53,656
Year 9	5,000	45,000	62,468
Year 10	5,000	50,000	71,853

The halfway point of value creation would be $71,853÷2 = $35,926. It can be seen that this occurs between year 5 ($30,317) and year 6 ($37,612). By interpolation, we can determine that the halfway point occurs at 5.77 years. So the last half of value creation occurs within the last 4.23 years, or 42%, of the investment period.

Now consider another scenario in which the investor, benefitting from a rising salary, increases his contributions by $500 per year. The value creation now looks like this:

End of:	Contribution	Accumulated Contributions	Total Value
Year 1	$5,000	$5,000	$5,325
Year 2	5,500	10,500	11,528
Year 3	6,000	16,500	18,667
Year 4	6,500	23,000	26,802
Year 5	7,000	30,000	35,999
Year 6	7,500	37,500	46,325
Year 7	8,000	45,500	57,857
Year 8	8,500	54,000	70,669
Year 9	9,000	63,000	84,847
Year 10	9,500	72,500	100,479

The halfway point of value creation would be $100,479÷2 = $50,239. This point now occurs somewhat later than the first example – between years 6 and 7. We can calculate this point as 6.34 years.

Here the last half of value creation occurs during the last 3.66 years, or 37%, of the investment life.

Now consider a final example in which the investor increases his contributions each year and also receives $20,000 from an inheritance or perhaps the sale of real estate later in life:

End of:	Contribution	Accumulated Contributions	Total Value
Year 1	$5,000	$5,000	$ 5,325
Year 2	5,500	10,500	11,528
Year 3	6,000	16,500	18,667
Year 4	6,500	23,000	26,802
Year 5	7,000	30,000	35,999
Year 6	7,500	37,500	46,325
Year 7	8,000	45,500	57,857
Year 8	28,500	74,000	91,969
Year 9	9,000	83,000	107,532
Year 10	9,500	92,500	124,638

The halfway point now is $124,638÷2 = $62,319. This point occurs at 7.13 years. Now the last half of value creation occurs during the last 2.87 years, or 29%, of the total investment period.[5]

So here is the takeaway from these examples. If we make the basic, "real world" assumptions that portfolios are built gradually over time with increasing contributions, perhaps augmented by larger one-time events such as an inheritance or the sale of real estate/business assets in later years, then it becomes clear that our portfolio value reaches "critical mass" (defined as the halfway point) after – *and perhaps well after* – the halfway point of the investment period. So the second half of value creation will be concentrated within a smaller – *and perhaps much smaller* – period of time than the first half.

Now connect that conclusion back to the table on page 17. What if this critical smaller period of value creation – perhaps as short as 10 years before withdrawals begin – should have started around 1966? Or to bring the question up to date, what if this period started a few years before 2000? Or before 2008? If this critical period of value creation centered around those years and you were relying on your portfolio to expand to its full potential to fund your retirement, the results would have been exceptionally stressful and difficult and might have required very substantial changes in lifestyle.

In the real world, there are very few true long-term investors.

Nearly all of us who save over time will find that there is a small, critical period of time – "make or break" time – wherein our portfolios either grow quickly to a successful level or else

---

5   I have limited these three examples to ten years to simplify the presentation. However, I have included a much longer example which shows a 40-year investment period with increasing contributions (SEE **ATTACHMENT A**). This example gives us a half way point at 31.2 years, with the other half of value creation occurring within the last 8.8 years, or 22% of the full investment period.

falter, stagnate, and decline much more rapidly than we had an-ticipated. No matter how disciplined our savings pattern may be during the first 30 years or so of portfolio construction, no matter how carefully we may select and diversify our portfolio, no matter what experts we may listen to, if by sheer bad luck our portfolios reach critical mass at the wrong time, we are – well – we're screwed. Might as well just say it.

Portfolio Construction – or *Destruction?*

Assuming I can get away with that last sentence, let me give you some actual, real-world examples of *how screwed up your portfolio can actually get!*

I want to consider the investment results of eight investors who each managed to construct a portfolio of $500,000 with ten years remaining until retirement. They have reached critical mass and need solid investment performance over the next ten years to reach their goal of retiring with $1,000,000. They believe that this is a reasonable expectation, as they assume nominal annual growth of 6.5%, a conservative number given historical nominal growth rates around 8%. In addition, they are in a position to save and contribute $10,000 in additional funds every year to the portfolio – a total of $100,000 over the ten year period.

Given these realistic assumptions, these investors calculate that if this scenario plays out as expected, they should retire with a portfolio balance of $1,073,000.

The table below shows our eight investors, who reach retirement age in sequential years beginning in 2007 and ending in 2014. For each investor (column), the table shows the development of their portfolios beginning ten years prior to their retirement dates. The first column shows the actual price change (expressed as a multiple) of the S&P 500 Stock Index for each year from 1998 through 2014. *This is the actual, real-world performance that our investors would have experienced.* The ending portfolio value for each year is multiplied by the price change for the next year, and the sum of $10,000 is added to that new value to produce the closing yearend balance.

VALUE OF PORTFOLIO AT RETIREMENT SHOWN IN BOLD

PRICE		STARTING PORTFOLIO OF $500,000 — 10 YEARS PRIOR TO RETIREMENT							
		1997	1998	1999	2000	2001	2002	2003	2004
	1997	500							
1.267	1998	643	500						
1.195	1999	779	608	500					
0.899	2000	710	556	460	500				
0.870	2001	628	494	410	445	500			
0.766	2002	491	388	324	351	393	500		
1.264	2003	631	501	419	453	507	642	500	
1.090	2004	697	556	467	504	562	710	555	500
1.030	2005	728	582	491	529	589	741	582	525
1.136	2006	837	672	568	611	679	851	671	606
1.036	2007	**877**	706	598	643	714	892	705	638
0.615	2008		**444**	378	406	449	558	443	402
1.235	2009			**477**	511	565	700	558	507
1.126	2010				**585**	646	798	638	580
1.000	2011					**656**	808	648	590
1.133	2012						**926**	744	678
1.296	2013							**974**	890
1.115	2014								**1002**
CAGR		5.78%	-1.18%	-0.47%	1.58%	2.75%	6.35%	6.89%	7.20%
NET CAGR		4.51%	-3.67%	-2.78%	-0.30%	1.07%	5.15%	5.74%	6.08%

CAGR shows the Compound Average Growth Rate (CAGR) of the entire portfolio over the ten year period.

NET CAGR shows the CAGR of the portfolio excluding the $10,000 annual contributions.

The results are startling and dramatic.

- No investor – *not one* – reached the expected goal of $1,073,000.
- The last three investors come reasonably close to their goal, but the preceding four investors fell *far* short. Two of these four investors actually experienced negative returns, even after contributing $100,000 in additional funds to their portfolios.
- No investor achieved a NET CAGR (excluding contributions) return of 6.5%.
- The average NET CAGR over this eight year period was 1.98% – less than two percent.
- Average NET CAGR is actually negative for the first five years. The number becomes positive only because of the strong S&P performance over the past three years.

Focus for a minute on the highlighted row for 2008. Imagine how the last seven investors must have felt on December 31, 2008. *All but one had lost money.* Their portfolio balances were actually less than the initial $500,000, even after adding $10,000 per year.

I mention this because I wonder if these investors would have kept their money in the market at this point. I think the urge to sell and get out would have been extremely strong. I have a number of friends who bailed out at the height of the crash – a terrible decision in hindsight – *but who could have blamed them?* I think it would have taken nerves of steel to stay invested and still believe that you initial goal could be reached.

The above table is a clear and immediate reminder of the risks that can occur when a portfolio reaches critical mass. If during this relatively brief period the market moves against you – *and there is nothing you can do about this* – then your portfolio may fall short – *very, very short* – of your goals for retirement.

Think about the disappointment and the changes in lifestyle that four of our investors faced as they entered retirement with *60% or less* of the nest egg they had envisioned.

And this is not a hypothetical exercise. Real people went through this. And keep in mind that this is not ancient history – *this just happened!*

"Life looks just a little more mathematical and regular than it is. Its exactitude is obvious, but its inexactitude is hidden – its wildness lies in wait"

— *G. K. Chesterton, Historian, Poet, Philosopher, Theologian*

Entering Retirement –
The Ultimate Crap Shoot

Just as we saw the market damage a portfolio *in the making*, it can also upend a portfolio *already made*. Let's now take a look from another angle – the retiree's side – and see what happened to savers who did in fact reach their investment goals as they entered retirement between 1998 and 2007.

I am going to consider ten investors, each of whom reached critical investment mass and subsequently succeeded in building a substantial portfolio of $1,000,000 before retiring. These ten investors all retire at age 65 in sequential years beginning in 1998. They need to draw an initial annual amount of $60,000 from their portfolio to sustain their lifestyle. It is assumed that the inflation rate will be 2.0%.

Assuming that their portfolios will return 6.5% per year, our investors calculate that their portfolios should carry them for 32 years – to age 97 – before their funds are exhausted.[6] So everything seems to be in place for a secure and happy retirement.

These retirees are heavily invested in growth stocks that pay little or no dividends.

They are counting on continued price appreciation to fund their retirement.

The table below shows what would have happened to our ten investors – and I am sure actually did happen to numerous retirees – using S&P 500 Stock Index data for the period between 1998 and 2015:

---

6 Thanks to my nephew Pete, the math genius of the family, who built an Excel calculator to determine years to exhaustion.

REMEMBER: EACH INVESTOR STARTED WITH ONE MILLION DOLLARS

Retirement Date	Funds Remaining January 1, 2015	Funds Exhausted	Years Remaing to Exhaustion	Age at Fund Exhaustion
1998	$ 176,321		3	85
1999	$ 0	2013		80
2000	$ 0	2011		77
2001	$ 0	2014		79
2002	$ 362,971		5	83
2003	$ 1,074,976		24	101
2004	$ 720,494		13	89
2005	$ 689,869		13	88
2006	$ 757,729		15	89
2007	$ 662,834		13	86

See **ATTACHMENT B1** for data

I have looked at this table over a dozen times and I still shake my head. *This is crazy*! Here we have ten investors who did everything right – they were focused, disciplined, diligent, and they achieved their portfolio retirement goal – yet strictly and solely because of circumstances totally beyond their control:

Only one of the ten is expected to reach the original goal of fund exhaustion at age 97

Take a look at what happens here. The first four retirees are hit by the double train wreck of the dot.com crash (2000-2002) and then the giant collapse of 2008. The first retiree has a boost from the end of the '82 bull market, but is nearly broke by 2015. *The next three retirees are all completely wiped out.* The fifth retiree (2002) misses about half of the dot.com decline, but the recovery of 2003-2007 is not enough to stave off the effects of 2008. That investor has about five years of funding left by 2015.

But now look at retiree #6 (2003). This is the luckiest guy on the block! He completely misses the dot.com break, starts with a very strong market in 2003, and that gives him four solid years to build up enough of a reserve to withstand 2008. He comes through that with enough left to recoup everything and by 2015 he is back to his original investment. If in fact future market returns are 6.5% per year (as originally predicted), he will have 24 more years to go and remains solvent until the age of 101.

The last four retirees miss the boom year of 2003, so they come through 2008 in much worse shape. Assuming that they can in fact earn 6.5% per year going forward, they are all predicted to run out of money in their late '80s. That may be good enough, but it is still far short of their original goal of age 97.

This table captures the random, unpredictable nature of investing for price appreciation

Here are ten examples of savers who did everything right, yet only one manages to achieve a financially secure future. If lucky #6 had retired only two year earlier, he would have lost everything. Instead, he alone winds up in 2015 with more than his original amount.

ALL CHANCE
ALL RANDOM
ALL LUCK

Quite a bummer, if you ask me.
There must be a better way.
And there is.

Dividends

Dividends Defined

We have just reviewed a number of hypothetical scenarios to show how portfolios might have performed for investors who were approaching or entering retirement. We have focused on the past twenty years – 1995 to 2015 – to emphasize recent stock market performance: *This is what has just happened.* We have seen how comfortable statistics regarding steady, long term price appreciation simply collapse over the short term. Investors with identical portfolio profiles can be successful – or utterly destroyed – in reaching financial security by the simple timing difference of a year or two in reaching retirement age.

The scenarios presented above assume that investors are relying on stock price appreciation – *and the continuing sale of appreciated stock* – to provide the income they require. If this approach is taken, then the investor must succeed in "buying low and selling high" on a reasonably consistent basis. If the investor fails to do this, and is forced to sell stock in a down market to pay expenses, then *he has experienced a permanent loss of purchasing power.* As we will discuss later on, this is *the true definition of investment risk – a loss of purchasing power.* A security has been sold at a loss – it is gone forever can and never recover. *Game over!*

This therefore is the ultimate goal of Dividend Growth Investing: *Income.* We seek to develop a portfolio that *provides all the income we need without the necessity of selling stock.* If we can reach the goal of a 100% organic income portfolio, then *we can avoid permanent losses.* Sure, we will experience *unrealized* capital losses, but if we don't sell, these losses *will not become permanent.*

So the remainder of this book will be devoted to a study of the income produced by common stocks and by certain other securities that will be discussed in detail in the next section. Let's now take an overview of our primary income source – dividends.

What are Dividends?

To begin, dividends are paid by corporations. Corporations are distinct legal entities and are by far the most common form of large business ownership. When a corporation is formed, individuals contribute money and/or expertise to begin business operations, and in return receive shares of capital stock representing their percentage ownership of the business. To manage the company, shareholders elect a board of directors, which normally includes certain officers of the company and perhaps certain independent "outside" directors who are not employees of the business. Directors are ultimately responsible for all actions and activities undertaken by the corporation.

Once the corporation begins to generate a positive cash flow, the directors **may** elect to pay out some of this cash in the form of dividends to shareholders. And just to be clear, these payments – these dividends -- are real, cold, hard cash. Once the payments have been made, it is virtually impossible (other than cases of fraud or bankruptcy) that the shareholder would have to give them back. And once the directors begin such payments, it is usual that the dividends will continue to be paid, and hopefully increased, on a regular periodic basis.

Dividend Risk

It is important to pause at this point to emphasize that there is *no obligation or legal requirement of any kind that directors must declare and pay a dividend*. This decision is completely voluntary and is made only when the directors believe that such payments will not imperil the growth or financial strength of the company. It should be made clear that **the directors may eliminate or reduce a dividend at any time**. This

is the fundamental risk of Dividend Growth Investing. It is a real risk and it is always present and always a possibility.

The purpose of this book is therefore twofold: First, we will examine the benefits of Dividend Growth Investing and explain the basic principles – procedural and mathematical – that produce these benefits. Secondly, we will establish a check list – a protocol – *to select those stocks where we believe the danger of a dividend cut is significantly reduced.*

Managing Dividend Risk

How do we manage dividend risk? Here is a "sneak preview" of the protocol we will establish in considerable detail in Sections Three and Four:

- We will only consider those companies that have paid continuous dividends for a minimum period of ten years;
- We will exclude any company that has experienced a dividend cut within the past seven years;
- We will review and weigh the level of dividend growth over the past ten years;
- We will review and weigh the number of consecutive years that the dividend has been increased;
- We will only consider companies that have produced a record of earnings that comfortably cover the dividend payments;
- We will review and weigh the strength of the company's balance sheet;
- We will only consider companies with an Investment Grade rating from Standard and Poors;
- We will review and weigh the growth of Cash Flow from Operations;
- We will only select companies that have demonstrated a strong competitive position in their industries.

Does this check list eliminate dividend risk? **No it does not.** However, I can say that the protocol has worked very well for me over the past four years. I have purchased and sold nearly one hundred securities during this period and have experienced exactly two dividend cuts. Nevertheless, **this risk cannot be eliminated and is always present.**

Dividend Risk vs. Capital Gains Risk

We have set forth the basic risk of dividend investing, which is the risk of a dividend cut. It is important to point out that this *risk is limited and confined within the company itself and is not affected by forces or events that occur outside the company.* By this I mean that the broad forces that move the market as a whole do not impact the level of dividend cash that you receive. The only thing that can affect your dividend is an issue or problem that occurs within the company paying the dividend, and the subsequent decision of the board of directors that this problem warrants a dividend cut. *So your risk is **company specific**. It is not market inclusive.*

Now let us consider the risks that are involved in "growth" investing, which is just a short way of saying that the primary investment goal is capital gains. Our first risk, as with dividends, is company specific. We have to depend on a number of micro factors to generate capital gains, but the most basic is *growth of earnings.* If earnings decline, or if the market perceives that the earnings are likely to decline, then the price of the stock is likely to fall. *Note that the market determines this. This is not something that the board of directors can control.*

The risk of a decline in earnings could of course also affect dividend payments. But the difference with dividends is that this is a *board decision, not a market decision. So the board in effect serves as a buffer. Unless the earnings issue/problem is significant and/or prolonged, it is likely that the board will do its best to protect and preserve an established dividend track record* (discussed at greater length later in this section).

But there is another risk that growth investors face. In addition to the company specific risk of an earnings decline, there is another risk – perhaps even greater – *that the market as a whole may decline.* Or to put it in slightly more technical terms, the market may reduce the general level at which it values earnings – *the overall market price/earnings ratio may decline.*

Here is a simple equation that summarizes the two levels of risk that the growth investor faces:

$$P = (P/E) \times E$$

Where: P equals the price that you receive when you sell your stock;

P/E equals the price/earnings ratio at which the market values earnings;

E equals the earnings of the corporation.

If a dividend portfolio is 100% income organic, there is no need to sell stock to meet expenses.

But now consider the growth investor. Since he is not receiving direct cash, he *must sell stock to raise cash.* And there are two factors – not one – that determine how much cash he will receive. The first is company specific – the level of corporate earnings. Assuming for a minute that the market P/E remains steady, a decline in company earnings will cause the price of the stock to fall a certain amount. *But the market P/E is not steady, and this then creates a second layer of risk of additional loss.* The market P/E ratio will rise and fall depending on a host of factors, including:

- The stages of the business cycle;
- Changes in Federal Reserve policy, interest rates and/or inflation;

- US government taxation and deficit management issues;
- Domestic and foreign political developments;
- International economic developments;
- Sudden exogenous events (oil prices, natural disasters, terrorism, etc)

To summarize, the dividend investor and the growth investor both face the company specific risk of an earnings decline, although this risk plays out differently between the two parties. The dividend investor can only suffer a loss if the board of directors takes action, whereas the growth investor will be at the mercy of the market, with no possibility of a buffer provided by the company.

But the growth investor – and not the dividend investor – is then exposed to another fundamental risk: The risk of a general market decline. We have already seen how such precipitous declines in 2000-2002 and 2008 affected savers and investors, destroying the stock values of virtually all companies, *regardless of – and over and above – the strength of their earnings.* This second risk of loss is completely *beyond the control of both the investor and the companies he invests in.* There is simply nothing that can be done to avoid this!

So here is the ultimate decision that an investor has to make. There is always risk involved in investing.

Which set of risks would you choose to accept?

- Dividend Risk:
    1. Company specific risk only
    2. Controlled by Board of Directors
    3. Board may act as buffer to protect the dividend
    4. Not affected by market forces
    5. A 100% organic portfolio eliminates the need to sell stock

- Capital Gains Risk:
    1. Company specific **and** market inclusive risks
    2. Company earnings determine stock price, and:
    3. General market P/E ratio *also* determines stock price
    4. Market – not directors – determines the cash you get for your stock
    5. No buffer to protect investor from either form of risk
    6. Stocks must be sold to generate cash

For me, this choice has been an easy one to make. When you have completed this book, I think the choice will be an easy one for you as well.

"Trading is hazardous to your wealth."

— *Journal of Finance, April 2000*

Dividends: A First Look

Well, let's get back to our poor retirees.

I think they need a break.

Let's give them one.

Dividends.

Remember that our retirees were capital gains investors. They did not buy dividend stocks.

They – or their advisors – believed that they could buy low/ sell high to generate income. Because of that assumption, I used the Standard and Poors 500 Stock Index to project their portfolio performance. The S&P 500 is perhaps the most widely used index to measure broad market price movements, and it is appropriate to use this index as a proxy for portfolio performance due to price changes. However, this index *only reflects the returns produced by price appreciation. It does not include dividends.*

So now let us bring dividends into the picture. Let us now assume that our retirees invest broadly over the S&P 500 stocks, to *include those stocks in the index that pay dividends.* Generally the overall dividend yield on S&P 500 stocks varies around the 2.0% level, which does not seem particularly high. But I think you will be interested to see what that relatively small boost does for our ten investors.

Instead of the S&P 500 Index, we will now project portfolio results using the *S&P 500 Total Return Index.*

This index includes price appreciation *and* dividend payments, and assumes that all *cash dividends are reinvested back into the index.*

Since dividends paid by S&P 500 companies yield about 1.5%- 2.5% per year, annual changes in the S&P 500 Total Return

Index usually run about 1.5-2.5% higher than changes in the traditional S&P 500 index:

	S&P 500 Index:	% Change	S&P Total Return Index:	% Change
1997	970		1299	
1998	1229	26.7 %	1670	28.6 %
1999	1469	19.5	2021	21.0
2000	1320	-10.1	1837	-9.1
2001	1148	-13.0	1619	-11.9
2002	880	-23.4	1261	-22.1
2003	1112	26.4	1623	28.7
2004	1212	9.0	1799	10.8
2005	1248	3.0	1888	4.9
2006	1418	13.6	2186	15.8
2007	1468	3.6	2306	5.5
2008	903	-38.5	1453	-37.0
2009	1115	23.5	1837	26.4
2010	1257	12.6	2114	15.1
2011	1257	0.0	2159	2.1
2012	1426	13.3	2504	16.0
2013	1848	29.6	3316	32.4
2014	2059	11.5	3769	13.7

S&P Total Return Index: Chicago Board Options Exchange (cboe.com)

So using the S&P Total Return Index, we can restate the table for our retirees as follows (next page):

Retirement Date	S&P 500 Funds Remaining January 1, 2015	S&P 500 Age at Fund Exhaustion	S&P 500 Total Return Funds Remaining January 1, 2015	S&P 500 Total Return Age at Exhaustion	Age Gain
1998	$ 176,321	85	$ 601,190	91	6
1999	0	80	$ 134,115	82	2
2000	0	77	0	79	2
2001	0	79	$ 239,712	82	3
2002	$ 362,971	83	$ 688,889	90	7
2003	$ 1,074,976	101	$1,556,661	141*	40
2004	$ 720,494	89	$1,055,221	100	11
2005	$689,869	88	$ 977,038	97	9
2006	$757,729	89	$1,018,553	98	9
2007	$662,834	86	$ 866,740	92	6
Total Funds:	$ 4,445,194	Ave Age: 85.7	$7,138,119	Ave Age*: 91.6	

See **ATTACHMENT B2** for data   * 2003 set at 105 years

Look at the results we have achieved just by adding and re-investing a relatively modest dividend yield:

- Total funds remaining for all retirees as of January 1, 2015 increased 60.6% from $4.45MM to $7.14MM. This means that dividends were responsible for 38% of the total return, precisely in line with the percentage norm determined in various historical studies (See next chapter and footnote 8).
- The average age for portfolio exhaustion increased by 5.9 years, from 85.7 to 91.6. Note that the gain for year 2003 was substantially reduced to reflect a realistic age limit.
- Our first four retirees were still in pretty sad shape, given that all four experienced some or all of the double train wreck of 2000-2002 and 2008. Nevertheless there were still some small gains achieved.

- The last six retirees achieved substantial gains. Whereas only one retiree remained solvent at age 97 without dividends, now four of our investors reached that age. For this last group of five, the average increase in portfolio value due to dividends was 39.6%.

So here is our first look at the power of dividends – and recall that we are talking about a modest dividend yield of about 2% for the S&P 500.

But why stop at 2%?

Consider what our retirees would have achieved if at the moment of retirement, they had invested in solid, proven securities with a portfolio dividend yield of 6.0% that grew with inflation

No retiree would ever have had to sell a single share. Stock market price swings would no longer affect them.

THEY WOULD BE 100% ORGANIC

THEY WOULD HAVE ACHIEVED

CONTROL   *CONSISTENCY*   *COMFORT*

Dividends – The Way Out

As I mentioned at the beginning of this section, investors in my age group who first experienced the bull market of 1982 pretty much ignored the subject of dividends completely. At least that was true in my case. The hot stocks you really wanted to own – tech stocks, growth stocks, dot.com stocks – usually did not pay any dividends at all, so the subject was completely irrelevant there. But even if a stock did pay a dividend, the average yield then was about 3-4%, and with prices climbing, yields were dropping fast. So if the total return on stocks grew at a rate in excess of 16% per year, then capital gains were the primary cause of this growth and that's what held our attention.

But during the "lost decade" of 2000-2010, *there were no capital gains*, at least not at the aggregate market level. That was a decade-long shock to us bull market investors, and to some of us, it appeared that a new approach – an entirely new investment strategy – was necessary. The key characteristics of this new strategy – if we could find one – were that it must offer the investor:

- CONTROL over investment returns;
- CONSISTENT investment returns;
- COMFORT and relief from unavoidable price/value fluctuations

In particular, this strategy needed to address the whole question of market timing, which we have just discussed. If we worked for years to build a portfolio, how could we protect ourselves if, during the few very critical years of growth prior to the onset of withdrawals, the market moved against us?

Over the past several years I have done a great deal of reading and research on the subject of dividends. I could produce pages and pages of statistics, charts, and graphs that would establish the following conclusions:

- *Cash dividends are responsible for at least 40% of total stock returns.* If one considers the reinvestment of dividends, this percentage is much higher and can exceed 90% of total returns.
- *Dividend-paying stocks outperform non-dividend paying stocks on a total return basis.* Between 1972 and 2012, dividend payers achieved total annual returns well in excess of 8%, while non-payers yielded less than 2%.
- *Dividend-paying stocks produce less volatility than non-payers.*
- Among dividend-paying stocks, those *stocks with higher dividend yields and those that consistently increase dividend payments offer the highest total returns.*
- *Dividends are predictable.* Once a US company initiates a dividend payment, an implicit contract with shareholders is created that it makes it extremely painful for the company to cut or cease such payments.[7]

As important – crucial – as these preceding points may be, and as much as I appreciate the visual impact of charts and graphs, I am determined to keep this book focused and avoid the "TMI" (Too Much Information) trap that most investment books fall into. So I will ask the reader's indulgence to accept these points[8] so that I can move ahead with a single 20-year table that I think will make the central thesis of this book quite clear:

---

7   This is not necessarily true of foreign corporations and is the main reason that I tend to shy away from foreign stocks.

8   In my opinion, the best studies on dividend stock performance have been performed by Ned Davis Research, Inc., Venice, Florida. The quickest way to access these studies, which will confirm all of the five points listed above, is to Google "Ned Davis Dividend Study." This search will produce links to various articles produced by Nuveen Investments, Hartford Funds, JP Morgan Funds, Zacks.com, and other investment firms. All of these articles are based on the work of Ned Davis Research.

S&P 500 INDEX		DIVIDENDS				
As of December 31		Coca Cola	AT&T	Chevron	Clorox	HCP
1995	616	$0.22	$0.82	$0.96	$0.51	$1.07
1996	741	.25	.85	1.04	.56	1.15
1997	970	.28	.89	1.14	.61	1.23
1998	1229	.30	.94	1.22	.68	1.31
1999	1469	.32	.97	1.24	.76	1.39
2000	1320	.34	1.01	1.30	.82	1.47
2001	1148	.36	1.02	1.33	.84	1.55
2002	880	.40	1.07	1.40	.85	1.63
2003	1112	.44	1.16	1.43	.98	1.66
2004	1212	.50	1.25	1.54	1.08	1.67
2005	1248	.56	1.29	1.75	1.12	1.68
2006	1418	.62	1.33	2.01	1.16	1.70
2007	1468	.68	1.42	2.26	1.42	1.78
2008	903	.76	1.60	2.53	1.72	1.82
2009	1115	.82	1.64	2.66	1.92	1.84
2010	1257	.88	1.68	2.84	2.10	1.86
2011	1257	.94	1.72	3.09	2.30	1.92
2012	1426	1.02	1.76	3.51	2.48	2.00
2013	1848	1.12	1.80	3.90	2.70	2.10
2014	2059	1.22	1.84	4.21	2.90	2.18

Source: Longrundata.com

I remember the first time I looked at the Standard and Poor's Index numbers (left column). I was astounded then, just as I am astounded again as I prepare this table. Just look at the volatility! Frankly, it's amazing that anyone would want to invest in the stock market after seeing such results.

The table begins at the end of the 1982 bull market, which we have discussed. Beginning in 1995, the market (S&P 500) *doubles* over the next three years, and then increases another 20%

in 1999. This represents a compound growth rate of 24.3% over the four year period. This bull market sure went out with a bang!

But then the dot-com bubble begins to burst, and the market heads south in a hurry. The index falls 10% in 2000, 13% in 2001, and a whopping 23% in 2002. That represents a *negative* growth rate of 15.7% for the three year period. *All the gains of the past five years have been wiped out.*

But then the market begins to claw its way back. Consecutive gains are racked up over the next five years. The market is up 26% in 2003, 9% in 2004, 3% in 2005, 14% in 2006, and 4% in 2007. By the end of 2007, the S&P Index is *exactly* back to its level at the end of 1999, the end of the bull market. So – *no gain whatsoever for eight full years*, but at least we are back to square one.

Well, not so fast. We all know the next act of this play.

When the chaos of 2008 was finally – mercifully – over, the S&P index *had lost 38% of its value in one single year.* The market – once again – had wiped out all the gains of the past five years, *but also wiped out all the gains of the five years before that!* So in just one year, market value had retreated over a decade.

So beginning in 2009, and continuing through to today, the market is once again clawing its way back. It took another four years, but by 2013 the market had again regained its high level of 2007, which was the same level as 1999. *That's fourteen years with no gain. Zero.*

Can anyone really feel comfortable with this? I mean, this is not ancient history. We all lived through this – we all remember this. *This really did happen to us.* And while the last seven years have been good to investors and we have licked our wounds and moved on, I am *certainly* not about to believe that everything has been "cleaned up" and that we have seen the last of:

- Toxic mortgages
- Subprime lending

- Synthetic derivatives
- Reckless leverage
- Suspicious financial statements
- Questionable credit ratings
- Compromised regulators
- Billion dollar bailouts
- Good old fashioned, felonious, malfeasance!

So that is why I have adopted a new investment philosophy. And to understand the basic foundation of that philosophy, please go back to the table on page 45 and now look at the columns under dividends. Presented are the dividend histories of five American companies, all of which are well known (except perhaps HCP, which is a Real Estate Investment Trust (REIT) invested in health care facilities). All five companies are "dividend aristocrats" that have increased their dividends every year for at least 25 consecutive years.

As explained above, dividends are *real cash payments*, made every quarter or every month, that are paid directly into your brokerage account. These are NOT temporary or unrealized capital gains that can disappear at any moment. And here is the most important fact of all:

NO MATTER WHAT THE MARKET MAY DO, REAL CASH DIVIDEND PAYMENTS KEEP ROLLING IN!

"The fact that a nationwide spate of mortgage defaults _hadn't_ happened convinced investors that it _couldn't_ happen, and their certainy caused them to take actions so imprudent that it _had to_ happen."

— _Howard Marks, Chairman_
Oaktree Capital Management

What is clear from the table is that there is *no correlation whatsoever between the behavior of the market (S&P 500) and the behavior of these dividend payments.* The dividends – again, real cash payments – of these companies *not only continue* through the gyrations of the S&P, but:

- They increase every single year.
- They increase in a steady and consistent manner.
- They increase no matter what direction the market may take.
- They increase without regard to economic growth or recession.
- They increase even if the companies themselves experience a decline in earnings.

Here we see the results of companies that are truly shareholder friendly. These companies have made a firm commitment to create and perpetuate predictable, increasing, real cash flow for shareholders.

Here is the same table as presented just above, but instead of presenting absolute numbers or values, this table shows the percentage changes of such values between each year:

ANNUAL PERCENTAGE CHANGES

S&P 500 INDEX		DIVIDENDS				
As of December 31		Coca Cola	AT&T	Chevron	Clorox	HCP
1995	Start	Start	Start	Start	Start	Start
1996	20.3%	13.6%	3.7%	8.3%	9.8%	7.5%
1997	31.0	12.0	4.7	9.6	8.9	7.0
1998	26.7	7.1	5.6	7.0	11.4	6.5
1999	19.5	6.7	3.2	1.6	11.8	6.1
2000	-10.1	6.3	4.1	4.8	7.9	5.7
2001	-13.0	5.9	1.0	2.3	2.4	5.4
2002	-23.4	11.1	4.9	5.3	1.2	5.2
2003	26.4	10.0	8.4	2.1	15.2	1.8
2004	9.0	13.6	7.8	7.7	10.2	0.6
2005	3.0	12.0	3.2	13.6	3.7	0.6
2006	13.6	10.7	3.1	14.8	3.6	1.2
2007	3.6	9.7	6.8	12.4	22.4	4.7
2008	-38.5	11.8	12.7	11.9	21.1	2.2
2009	23.5	7.9	2.5	5.1	11.6	1.1
2010	12.6	7.3	2.4	6.8	9.4	1.1
2011	0.0	6.8	2.4	8.8	9.5	3.2
2012	13.3	8.5	2.3	13.6	7.8	4.2
2013	29.6	9.8	2.3	11.1	8.9	5.0
2014	11.5	8.9	2.2	7.9	7.4	3.8

Immediately you will notice that the only negative growth values occur with the S&P 500. The dividends paid by our five companies *always* have a positive growth rate, and within each company these growth rates are fairly stable from year to year. You can see that the percentage changes for dividends are far more stable than the changes for the S&P 500. The table may be summarized as follows:

	1995 - 2014 20 Year Growth Rates		1995 - 2014 Standard Deviation	Std Dev / Average (Coefficient of Variation)
	Average[9]	Compound[9]		
Standard & Poor's 500:	8.35%	6.56%	18.74%	2.24
Dividends:				
Coca Cola	9.46%	9.44%	2.46%	0.26
AT&T	4.38%	4.35%	2.85%	0.65
Chevron	8.14%	8.09%	4.03%	0.49
Clorox	9.69%	9.58%	5.50%	0.57
HCP	3.84%	3.81%	2.31%	0.60
All Five Companies:	7.10%	6.73%	4.36%	0.61

Forgive me. I have to get "mathy" for a minute. I will try to keep such outbursts to a minimum.

The Standard Deviation (STDEV) measures the volatility of a set of numbers by calculating the variation or dispersion of those numbers around the average. Many investors consider volatility to constitute the very definition of investment risk. Other investors use other definitions of risk. But regardless of the definition, *no one wants to see their returns jumping around all over the place.*

The ratio of STDEV / AVERAGE is in my opinion the best way to compare the volatility of two or more data sets. This ratio is known as the Coefficient of Variation (COV) and it is a relative metric that considers not just the STDEV alone, but relates STDEV to the average for comparative purposes. For example, Coca Cola and HCP both have similar low STDEV numbers, but Coke has a much higher average. Therefore, Coke has

9   Please see **ATTACHMENT C** for a discussion of Average Growth Rate, Weighted Average Growth Rate, and Compound Average Growth Rate.

a much *lower COV, indicating lower volatility* relative to HCP.

Now look at the COV column. The COV for the S&P 500 is calculated at 2.24. This number is over eight times higher – *eight times more volatile* – than the COV of Coca Cola dividends. Taking all five stocks as a single data set, the COV of the S&P 500 is 3.7 times higher – 3.7 times more volatile – than this "mini portfolio" of stock dividends.

So if one looks at these five stocks – or dozens and dozens of other quality dividend stocks – this clear pattern emerges. *Dividend stocks produce low volatility, steady, consistent payments to you – cold, hard cash – in your account every month or every quarter.* Not only are they consistent, but these cash payments grow every single year. The management of such companies makes a commitment to its shareholders that it will protect the dividend as a very high priority, and will continue dividend increases even in the face of recession, tight credit, declining earnings, intense competition, or capital expenditures. In short:

> **Dividend payments are far more dependable than stock price appreciation.**

> **Dividends provide reliable growth with low volatility.**

> **Dividends provide the control we need to achieve consistent investment results**

> **DIVIDENDS OFFER US THE BASIS OF A NEW INVESTMENT PHILOSOPHY.**

"Most of financial history has taken place within two standard deviations.

"Everything interesting has occurred outside of two standard deviations."

— *Ric Kayne, Investor*

How Does Dividend Growth Investing Work?

Let's review what we have covered so far:

- Investors tend to save gradually increasing amounts over time, with possible bulk additions – usually coming later in life – from inheritances or the sale of real estate or business assets.
- It may take a significant number of years for a portfolio to reach the halfway point of value creation ("critical mass"). However, the second half of value creation may occur in an accelerated period of time that may last perhaps only 10 years or so before withdrawals begin.
- The timing of this accelerated period therefore becomes very critical. If the market is strong, then all may be well and the portfolio will reach its expected full value. But if the investor, through sheer bad luck, enters this critical period in a weak market, the portfolio may stagnate, weaken, and never reach its full potential before withdrawals become necessary.
- The recent twenty year history of stock market performance clearly shows a most erratic pattern that could easily upend the value creation of any investor unlucky enough to encounter a period of sustained or precipitous market decline.
- On the other hand, dividend paying companies tend to produce a very strong and steady pattern of increasing cash payments. These payments exhibit very low volatility and are quite predictable.

So instead of "rolling the dice" and hoping that volatile capital gains will carry the day, wouldn't it make sense to adopt an investment approach that centers on the consistency of dividends?

The answer is yes!

But how does dividend growth investment work?

Let's begin by considering three different scenarios in which an investor could receive dividend income.

Assume that $10,000 is invested to buy 100 shares with an initial dividend of $3.00/share (3% yield).

Scenario #1: Stable Dividend without Reinvestment

We assume that the dividend rate does not increase and that dividend payments are not reinvested.

Period	Cumulative Dividends	Yield @ Cost/ End of Period
Start		3.00%
5 Years	$ 1,500	3.00%
10 Years	3,000	3.00%
15 Years	4,500	3.00%
20 Years	6,000	3.00%

Scenario #2: Increasing Dividend without Reinvestment

Now the dividend increases at year end at an annual rate of 5.0%. Dividends are not reinvested.

Period	Cumulative Dividends	Yield @ Cost/ End of Period
Start		3.00%
5 Years	$ 1,657	3.64%
10 Years	3,773	4.65%
15 Years	6,473	5.94%
20 Years	9,919	7.58%

Scenario #2 exposes us to the *power of compound interest*. We start with a dividend amount of $300.00 in year 1. This amount increases 5% in year 2 to $315.00. That amount in turn increases 5% in year 3 to $330.75. The process continues until the annual dividend ultimately equals $758.07 by year 20. Note that this gives us a yield on our original cost ($10,000) of 7.58%, an amount that is more than twice the 3.00% final yield of scenario #1. Cumulative dividends after 20 years are 65% higher with scenario #2.

Scenario #3: Increasing Dividend *with* Reinvestment

Dividends grow 5% per year. Dividends are now reinvested to buy additional shares of stock. It is assumed that the price of the stock remains constant (each new share costs $100).

Period	Cumulative Dividends	Yield@ Cost/End of Period
Start		3.00%
5 Years	$ 1,771	4.14%
10 Years	4,480	6.43%
15 Years	8,834	10.55%
20 Years	16,279	18.51%

PLEASE TAKE A FEW MOMENTS TO LOOK CAREFULLY AT SCENARIO #3.

THIS IS THE MOST IMPORTANT TABLE PRESENTED IN THIS BOOK.

THIS IS WHAT DIVIDEND GROWTH INVESTMENT IS ALL ABOUT

Scenario #1 is a "steady state" scenario. The dividend remains constant and there is no reinvestment.

Nothing changes and nothing grows.

Scenario #2 introduces the power of compounding. Now the dividend grows at a rate of 5% per year.

The result is a substantial increase in total income
and yield at cost.

SCENARIO #3 INTRODUCES
ACCELERATED COMPOUNDING

Scenario #3 shows us what happens when we *combine dividend growth with dividend reinvestment.*

We have in effect doubled down on compounding. Dividends are growing at a compound rate, and with dividend reinvestment, the number of shares we own is also growing at a compound rate. And look at the results! After 20 years, cumulative dividends total $16,279, 2.7 times more than scenario #1 and 1.6 times more than scenario #2. Yield at cost finishes at 18.51%, a full 6 times higher than scenario #1 and well over twice the level of scenario #2.

So here is the simple power of Dividend Growth Investing:

Three basic forces are at work

that create and drive an accelerating rate of wealth creation

Increasing Dividends

Reinvestment of Dividends

Compound Interest

That's all there is to it!

Now let's take a look at the real world and a real example of Dividend Growth Investing in action.

The table below shows AT&T dividend and price history for the past twenty years. The table is a bit complicated but I want you to see – year by year – exactly what is happening and how DGI works.

AT&T DIVIDEND/PRICE HISTORY					
Year	Opening Shares	Dividend	Price	New Shares	Closing Shares
1995	1000.0	$ .82	$28.63	28.6	1028.6
1996	1028.6	.85	25.94	33.7	1062.3
1997	1062.3	.89	36.63	25.8	1088.1
1998	1088.1	.92	53.63	18.7	1106.8
1999	1106.8	.96	48.75	21.8	1128.6
2000	1128.6	1.01	47.75	23.9	1152.5
2001	1152.5	1.02	39.17	30.0	1182.5
2002	1182.5	1.07	27.11	46.7	1229.2
2003	1229.2	1.17	26.07	55.2	1284.4
2004	1284.4	1.25	25.77	62.3	1346.7
2005	1346.7	1.29	24.49	70.9	1417.6
2006	1417.6	1.33	35.75	52.7	1470.3
2007	1470.3	1.42	41.56	50.2	1520.5
2008	1520.5	1.60	28.50	85.4	1605.9
2009	1605.9	1.64	28.03	94.0	1699.9
2010	1699.9	1.68	29.38	97.2	1797.1
2011	1797.1	1.72	30.24	102.2	1899.3
2012	1899.3	1.76	33.71	99.2	1998.5
2013	1998.5	1.80	35.16	102.3	2100.8
2014	2100.8	1.84	33.59	115.1	2215.9

Sources: Prices: Morningstar.com   Dividends: Longrundata.com

First of all you will notice that the dividend amount increases every year. These are the actual dividends paid and over the past 20 years AT&T dividends increased at a compound growth rate of 4.35%. This is a solid rate of growth but by no means unusual for the quality dividend-paying companies that we will analyze later in this book.

Secondly, we are assuming that these dividends are reinvested to buy new shares. We have used the actual year-end stock price to determine for each year how many new shares we can buy.

The table begins with an investor buying 1000 shares of AT&T on January 1, 1995 at a price of $20.19 (not shown above) for a total initial investment of $20,190 (I am excluding transaction costs). The investor enrolls in the AT&T DRIP (Dividend Reinvestment Plan). His dividend in 1995 was $.82 per share, or $820.00 on 1000 shares. This was automatically invested at the year-end price of $28.63, so he acquired $820÷$28.63 = 28.6 new shares, creating a new balance of 1028.6 shares at year end.

Carrying this process forward until the end of 2014, our investor winds up with a total of 2215.9 shares. This represents an increase of 121.6% in the number of shares, more than doubling the original amount. And just to be clear, this growth did not require a single cent of additional investment after the original purchase twenty years before. *Every penny earned is the result of dividend growth and reinvestment.*

Here is a summary of the cumulative AT&T dividends received, showing the difference between dividend reinvestment (shown above) vs. non-reinvestment (not shown):

| Period | Cumulative Dividends | | End Of Period Yield On Cost | |
	Reinvestment	Non-reinvestment	Reinvestment	Non-reinvestment
Start			4.06%	4.06%
5 Years	$ 4,703	$ 4,440	5.26%	4.75%
10 Years	11,328	9,960	7.95%	6.19%
15 Years	22,104	17,240	13.04%	8.12%
20 Years	38,857	26,040	19.14%	9.11%

Like our hypothetical scenarios shown above, this real world example demonstrates the very core foundation of what makes DGI work. *If you combine dividend growth with dividend reinvesting, you have created a double growth stimulus.* Even without reinvesting, a rising dividend alone would cause total income and yield to experience geometric growth through compound interest. But when you add dividend reinvestment into the mix, you accelerate the compound growth factor and achieve a substantial increase in wealth accumulation.

So let me bring this full circle. If you invest with a primary focus on obtaining capital gains – buying low and selling high – there is ultimately no way that you – or your investment advisors – can control the outcome. No matter how carefully your stocks are selected, reviewed, or rebalanced, if the market is tanking – over which you have absolutely no control – your stocks are going to tank as well. You may be able to minimize the damage with some form of hedging strategy, but you are still going down. And if you are forced to sell in a down market, you will never regain that loss and you will have suffered a permanent decline in wealth – *a decline in purchasing power.* That is Warren Buffet's definition of risk – not volatility but *loss of purchasing power* – and that is exactly what an income approach to investing seeks to avoid.

Look again at the AT&T example above. Suppose that the price of AT&T stock had actually *fallen* during that 20 year period. Obviously this would have destroyed wealth in terms of the value of the stock. So the capital gains investor, who had spent or failed to reinvest his dividends, would clearly be worse off. But ironically, the DGI investor would be *better* off. How? *Because he would have been able to buy more shares at lower prices.* So his income stream would actually be *higher.*

This clearly seems counterintuitive. Who would ever want to see stock prices decline? Well, you never would if you focused on capital gains. But DGI investors may actually welcome market corrections, assuming that they have money to invest, because lower prices mean you can acquire *more dividend shares at higher yields.* The result is durable, predictable, higher income.

Let me be honest here. I like the idea of acquiring stock at a lower price/higher yield, but I will certainly never root for stock prices to go down in order to accomplish that. But if prices do fall, I have both the intellectual and emotional backstop of knowing that:

- I am in control of the income stream I need to fund my retirement;
- I have established a consistent and reliable cash flow;
- I have the comfort of a Sleep-Well-At-Night (SWAN) portfolio.

The AT&T Story: A True Case Study

I picked AT&T to demonstrate the power of Dividend Growth Investing, and by happy coincidence, so did Josh Peters, editor of Morningstar's monthly dividend newsletter. In his book "The Ultimate Dividend Playbook" – which I highly recommend – Josh writes a true story about one of his early clients, a woman who ultimately amassed a substantial portfolio. Josh traced her portfolio back over 40 years to find the secret of her success. He writes as follows:

> "I finally found the root of Marjorie's wealth: a handful of gifts of AT&T stock given to her by her father between 1955 and 1962. Their original value was $6,626. Very early on, she signed up for AT&T's dividend reinvestment plan. Instead of getting penny-ante dividend checks every three months, she turned those payments into additional shares, which led to more dividends, and so on. As AT&T prospered and raised its dividend rate, the value of each share rose as well – as did the Baby Bells' dividends and share prices. By 1999, this investment had blossomed into a portfolio of ten separate stocks worth more than $1 million – all of them descendants of the original Ma Bell.
>
> "I was astounded. Here was all this wealth, but Marjorie hadn't lifted a finger to earn it. Her account was marked by a distinct lack of active management ... She just held and held, reinvesting every dividend, letting these rising dividend payments do all of the work
>
> "I'm willing to bet that Marjorie's long-term investment record beats the vast majority of investors over the past half century."
>
> — Josh Peters, *The Ultimate Dividend Playbook*,
> John Wiley & Sons, 2008, p. XV

Here is another quote from Josh's book (p. IX), a perfect thought to end the first section of this book:

"You may have heard that the basic idea of the stock market is to buy low and sell high. Pardon me for saying so, but that sounds like a lot of work. An investment represents money that is supposed to work for me, right? Having earned my money once already, why should I have to work for it all over again?

"The trouble with this mentality – in addition to the poor odds of consistent success, of course – is that it puts almost 100% of the responsibility for profits on the back of the shareholder rather than the stock. It's as though the stock market is not about business at all, but rather a grand game pitting wily investors against each other in attempts to beat the market.

"But if we are to shed the game mentality of our fellow investors, our stocks must provide an alternative source of reward. Rewards with no additional effort. Rewards not subject to the whims of Wall Street.

"Above all, rewards paid in cash.

"*These rewards are cash dividends.*"

Amen, Josh!

Investing in a Down Market

Four pages ago I made the statement that dividend growth investors can actually "do better" when stock prices are falling. Of course I do not mean "better" in the sense of a higher portfolio value. But I *do* mean better in terms of achieving our primary investment goal – more income!

This appears to mean that dividend growth investors can have their cake and eat it too – that we win no matter what the market is doing. Well, if in fact you have a 100% organic portfolio – which along with other sources provides all the income you need to live on – and you also have some spare cash, *then this is exactly the case.*

Let's go back to our old friend AT&T and look at the first five years of our table. Here we see the actual results of reinvesting dividends. If we multiply opening shares by that year's dividend, we get a good approximation of the cash dividends received over this five year period:

AT&T DIVIDEND **ACTUAL** PRICE HISTORY						
Year	Opening Shares	Dividend	Price	New Shares	Closing Shares	Dividends
1995	1000.0	$ .82	$28.63	28.6	1028.6	$ 820.00
1996	1028.6	.85	25.94	33.7	1062.3	874.31
1997	1062.3	.89	36.63	25.8	1088.1	945.45
1998	1088.1	.92	53.63	18.7	1106.8	1001.05
1999	1106.8	.96	48.75	21.8	1128.6	1062.53
				128.6		$4,703.34

So after five years we wind up owning an additional 128.6 shares and receiving $ 4,703.34 in dividends.

For the most part share prices were increasing during this period, the end of the Great Bull Market.

Now let us change the table and *assume that share prices were declining* during the period:

AT&T DIVIDEND / **HYPOTHETICAL** PRICE HISTORY						
Year	Opening Shares	Dividend	Price	New Shares	Closing Shares	Dividends
1995	1000.0	$ .82	$25.00	32.8	1032.8	$ 820.00
1996	1032.8	.85	22.00	39.9	1072.7	877.88
1997	1072.7	.89	20.00	47.7	1120.4	954.70
1998	1120.4	.92	18.00	57.3	1177.6	1030.76
1999	1177.6	.96	16.00	70.6	1248.2	1130.50
				248.2		$4,813.84

So this hypothetical example shows us what is just a simple mathematical fact: As share prices fall, our reinvested dividends can buy more shares, increasing our dividend income, enabling us to buy more shares, and so the cycle continues. While this five-year example shows only a modest increase in income, take note that we have added 248.2 shares compared with 128.6 in the first table, a 93% increase. Compound interest will continue to do its work, as the increase in dividend income becomes larger between each year moving forward.

And even if your portfolio is not 100% organic and you do have to sell securities to pay expenses, you are still better off in that every dollar of additional income you receive is one dollar less in stocks that must be sold.

We do not focus on the <u>value</u> of the shares we own.

We focus on the <u>number</u> of shares that we own.

Summary: Section One

Investors who rely on price appreciation – capital gains – to fund retirement will always be exposed to significant risk. A sharp or prolonged market break can severely damage or possibly wipe out investment portfolios either in the making or already made. The twin market train wrecks of 2000-02 and 2008 clearly show us the danger of relying on a steady, stable increase in market pricing. Anyone entering retirement just before or during the opening years of this century saw their financial security devastated by forces utterly beyond their control. This is not ancient history. *This just happened!*

Dividends offer a way out.

The payment of real cash dividends is far more stable and predictable than the price behavior of the securities market. There are dozens of strong, quality US corporations that have demonstrated a convincing commitment to their shareholders to increase dividend payments each and every year regardless of market or economic conditions. By reinvesting these growing dividends, shareholders enjoy a double compound growth stimulus that accelerates wealth creation. Ironically, this wealth creation actually *increases* during market corrections, since more stock can be acquired at higher yields.

Why Dividend Growth Investing?
Here is my own bottom line.

Our investment portfolio consists of 50 securities with a yield at cost of 6.32%. These are all quality companies that have been carefully screened through a demanding and conservative protocol. As these companies increase their dividends, I have every confidence that this yield will increase enough to keep

pace with, or to exceed, the rate of inflation. And most important of all:

We are 100% organic.
All our living and income tax expenses are covered.

As long as we stay on budget and inflation remains under
control, then:

We should never have to sell a single share of stock.
We no longer worry about market price fluctuations.

We are in control.
We are receiving consistent returns.

Control + Consistency = Comfort

This book proposes and investment strategy
In which the investor succeeds
When he <u>buys</u> a stock
Rather than when he <u>sells</u> it

SECTION TWO

WHAT

"Time is a scarce and precious resource – not at all different from money. Focusing on what you can't control wastes it, focusing on what you can maximizes its value."

— *Investment Pancake*
Seeking Alpha.com contributor
July 14, 2015

What This Section Will Cover

Before we begin to construct a Dividend Growth portfolio, we need to know what can go in it!

This section will describe the various types of securities ("asset classes") that the typical individual investor might want to consider for selection in an organic portfolio. We will concentrate on securities that provide high yields and that increase cash payouts on an annual – or more frequent – basis.

These securities include:

- C corporations: Common Stock
- C Corporations: Preferred Stock
- Real Estate Investment Trusts (REITs)
- Master Limited Partnerships (MLPs)
- Funds: Open End, Closed End, Exchange Traded
- Business Development Companies
- High Yield Bonds
- Municipal Bonds

This section will review the purpose, structure, strengths/ weaknesses, and taxation issues related to each asset type. In the following sections we will discuss how to evaluate these securities, when to buy them, and how to integrate them to provide proper diversification within the entire portfolio.

You may notice that I do not include US government or investment grade corporate bonds in the above list. The reason is simple: I don't own any of these. There are two basic reasons for that: First, the interest rates now offered on these securities are quite low, and second, the great majority of these rates are fixed, so there is no yield growth. So unless you want to bet that interest rates will *fall* causing bond prices to *rise* (back to seeking capital gains!), then I see no reason to hold these securities.

I should make clear that my decision to hold no government or investment grade bonds flies in the face of conventional money management advice. Investment advisors point out that bonds offer a hedge against the volatility of stocks and hold up better in down markets. I won't argue against that, but that point is a low priority for income investors, *because our philosophy and approach is to maximize income and income growth from solid, proven companies* – that is our goal, rather than worrying about the price correlation, or lack of correlation, between various asset classes. Since Investment grade bonds do not conform to my investment strategy, *I just don't own them.* To do so would mean sacrificing too much income, to the point where it might *endanger a 100% organic portfolio that covers my living expenses.*

C Corporations: Common Stock

A corporation is one of the three basic forms of business structure and ownership. The vast majority of publically traded companies are structured as C corporations.

Under law, a corporation is considered a separate entity – in effect a person – separate from its owners, who become shareholders. Common shareholders vote in direct proportion to their share holdings and elect a board of directors, who are directly responsible for the affairs of the company.

There are two major advantages to the corporate form of ownership. First, shareholders are not personally responsible for the debts or obligations of the corporation. The most a shareholder can lose is the amount he has invested to acquire stock. Second, the corporation does not "die" when its shareholders do, but rather has an indefinite life that can only be terminated by legal action. These two factors are completely different from the proprietorship or general partnership form of ownership, wherein the business entity does *not* have a separate legal status, the owners are personally liable for all business debts, and the business expires with its owners.

In a sense, owning common stock offers "the best of both worlds," because the shareholder has limited downside risk, but unlimited potential gain. If the company takes off, only the shareholder can claim the profits. Bondholders will only get their fixed interest and principal payments, no matter how profitable the company may become. The corporation therefore becomes the perfect vehicle to raise the amount of capital – sometimes very substantial – necessary to commence or to expand a business enterprise.

A C corporation, like an individual, must pay taxes. Corporate profits are taxed first at the corporate level, and a second time when they are disbursed as dividends to shareholders. This "double taxation" has always been an issue for shareholders, although this issue was mitigated somewhat in 2003 when "qualified" dividends became subject to the same favored personal tax rates as long-term capital gains. A common dividend is considered "qualified" if the stock has been held for at least 61 days.[10]

Dividends are declared periodically (most C corporations declare quarterly) by the company's board of directors. It is important to recognize that many corporations pay no dividends at all and that *there is no legal requirement of any kind to declare and pay a dividend.* The board makes this decision completely at its sole discretion after reviewing the overall financial health and performance of the corporation. However, in this country, once a major company begins to pay a dividend, an implied contract arises between the company and its shareholders in which *it is expected that the dividends will continue, and further, that the dividends will increase.* This expectation is strong enough so that in many cases a company will continue its dividend, or even increase its dividend, even if the overall economy is weak, the stock market is tanking, or the company's own earnings have declined. In fact, the majority of the companies we will consider for purchase continued to increase their dividends right through the financial disaster of 2008, regardless of the extraordinary pressures brought to bear on board members during this period.

The investment community has traditionally categorized/sorted common stocks in two ways:

---

10   Technically, the stock must be owned for at least 61 days out of the 121-day period that began 60 days before the Ex-dividend date (OK, this is very confusing. See page 76.)

Valuation

When sorting stocks by valuation, companies are placed in a 3X3 grid, which includes market capitalization on the vertical axis and valuation type (value, core, growth) on the horizontal axis.

Definitions:

Large Cap: Stocks with a total market value in excess of $10 billion

Mid Cap: Stocks with a total market value of $2 billion to $10 billion

Small Cap: Stocks with a total market value of $300 million to $2 billion

Value Stocks: Established companies with slower growth. Most are dividend payers.

Growth stocks: Younger companies experiencing rapid growth. Fewer dividend payers.

Core stocks: Companies with some value and some growth characteristics

The grid looks like this:

Value	Core	Growth	
30	20	8	Large Cap
14	13	2	Mid Cap
11	1	1	Small Cap

Dividend Growth Investors will tend to concentrate on stocks located in the upper left-hand corner. These are the larger, more stable, dividend payers. The numbers in the grid show the percentage distribution of securities held in my own portfolio.

Sector

Here stocks are sorted into three basic sectors: Cyclical, Sensitive, and Defensive. These sectors are in turn divided into sub-sectors as follows:

Cyclical	Sensitive	Defensive
Basic Materials	Communication	Consumer Defensive
Consumer Cyclical	Energy	Healthcare
Financial Services	Industrials	Utilities
Real Estate	Technology	
26%	40%	34%

In general, DGI investors will have somewhat less cyclical and somewhat more defensive stocks. The percentages shown above represent the distribution of stocks in my own portfolio.

Regarding dividend payments, there are four important dates that we need to define:

Declaration Date:
The date upon which the board of directors declares that a dividend will be paid at some future date.

Ex-Dividend Date:
The first day upon which and after which a buyer of the stock will NOT be entitled to the next dividend. The Ex-Dividend date is usually two business days before the Record Date.

Record Date:
The date upon which all registered owners become entitled to the upcoming dividend.

Payable Date:
The date when the dividend is actually paid into your brokerage account.

An example might help to make this clear. The directors of

company ABC declare on May 1 that a dividend of $1.00/share will be paid to shareholders of record on May 20. The payment date is June 10.

May 1 is the Declaration Date.

Anyone who buys the stock up to and including May 17 will be entitled to receive this dividend.

Anyone who buys the stock on or after May 18 (Ex-Dividend date) will *not* be entitled to the dividend.

The Ex-Dividend date is two business days before the Record date.

The Record Date is May 20. All registered owners of the stock on this date will receive the dividend.

This allows 3 business days to settle the last permitted purchase (May 17) and become a shareholder of record by May 20.

The $1.00/share cash dividend is received in your brokerage account on June 10.

As discussed above, *the reinvestment of dividends is an essential component of wealth creation*. The easiest way to accomplish this is to "DRIP" your dividends, which means to enroll in an automatic Dividend Reinvestment Plan with each company. However, you may wish to let dividends accumulate and then open a new position or strengthen an existing position depending on your outlook for those securities at that point in time. But either way, *put those dividends back to work!*

Before leaving the general subject of common stock dividends, I would like to mention again the dividend studies performed by Ned Davis Research. These studies are cited by numerous investment firms to support the conclusions that:

- Over time dividends have been responsible for at least 40% of total stock returns;

- Reinvesting dividends increases this percentage up to 90% of total returns;
- Dividend stocks out-perform non-dividend stocks on a total return basis;
- Dividend stocks are less volatile than non-dividend stocks;
- Stocks with higher yields and stocks with increasing dividends produce the best total returns.

These studies are extremely important to Dividend Growth Investors and I would encourage you to review them. If you Google "Ned Davis Dividend Study" you will find links to various articles based on these studies. These studies help solidify the comfort of a "Sleep Well At Night" dividend portfolio!

C Corporations: Preferred Stock

Preferred stock is something of a hybrid security, combining features of both stocks and bonds. Like common stock, it represents equity ownership in a company. But whereas common stock does not necessarily pay a dividend, preferred stock virtually always does, and the preferred dividend must be paid before the common dividend is paid. In some cases the preferred dividend is *cumulative*, meaning that all cumulative preferred dividends that have been omitted and not paid must be paid in total before any common dividends may be paid.

Like a bond, the preferred dividend is set at a negotiated fixed rate, and preferred shares usually have no voting rights. Preferred stock is senior to common stock in liquidation, but junior to bondholders.

Preferred stock may be *convertible* into a predetermined number of common shares. If this feature is present, the exchange may occur at any time the investor chooses, regardless of the market price of the common stock. This offers some upside potential for the investor, as *straight* (non-convertible) preferred issues offer virtually no potential for capital gain based on future company earnings growth.[11]

Preferred stock may be *callable*, meaning that the company has the right to retire (prepay) a preferred issue, usually in the event that interest rates decline. In such a case, the company may wish to refinance the preferred issue at the lower rate. The redemption price may be set at a premium to par value in order to offer some call protection to the investor.

As with common stocks, preferred dividends become "qualified"

---

11   Like bonds, the market value of preferred stock is inversely related to the level of interest rates. See discussion in High Yield Bonds.

for capital gains tax treatment after a required holding period. This period is 91 days, compared to 61 days for common stock.

Since preferred stock dividends are fixed, this represents a negative factor for dividend growth investors. However, preferred dividends are often attractive on an absolute basis, frequently yielding over 5-6%. Due to liquidity and analysis constraints, I prefer to own preferred stocks through the purchase of certain closed-end investment funds, which provide broad sector diversification as well as higher leveraged yields (See further discussion under closed-end funds in this section).

Real Estate Investment Trusts

Real Estate Investment Trusts (REITs) offer an attractive opportunity for income investors. These securities offer high yields, as they are required by regulation to pay substantial dividends. Income is generated under legal rental contracts, so cash flow is steady and consistent. Contrary to common opinion, these securities generally do well in periods of rising interest rates and inflation. REITs are cyclical, and their dividends are usually treated as ordinary income.

REITs were created as a new asset class by federal legislation in 1960. The primary objective of this legislation was twofold: First, to enable individual investors to participate in the ownership of large-scale commercial real estate properties, and second, to create a diversified investment structure for real estate similar to the diversification provided by mutual funds for common stocks.

A key feature of REITs is that they are exempt from federal taxation. Therefore REITs avoid the double taxation problem that exists for regular C corporations. The dividends which REITs pay are taxed at the level of the investor who receives them. These dividends are normally not Qualified Dividends, meaning that they are taxed as ordinary income regardless of the holding period.

In return for their favored tax status, REITs are required to pay out 90% of their net income to their shareholders. However, this requirement is not quite as onerous as it may appear. Many REITs report very low net income, or even net losses, primarily because of depreciation. Depreciation is a very significant expense for REITs and dramatically reduces net income, but *it is a non-cash expense and therefore has no effect on cash flow.* So some REITs in fact pay out more than reported net income to shareholders.

There are two types of REITs. The great majority (90%) of REITs are *Equity REITs,* which own and lease (or operate) virtually any type of large-scale commercial property, including office buildings, shopping malls, hotels, health care properties, warehouses, apartments, storage centers, industrial buildings, movie and entertainment centers, sport and recreational facilities, and so forth. Some "pure play" REITs specialize in a certain *type* of property (for example, nursing homes) while most invest in a certain *class* of property (for example, retail). It would be rare for a REIT to have no focus at all and invest in a random group of properties. REITs normally seek diversification by geography, type of property, lease term, and number of tenants.

A much smaller number (10%) of REITs are *Mortgage REITs,* or mREITs. These companies do not own real estate, but rather lend money to commercial property owners through mortgages and loans that are usually secured by a lien on the property. As mortgage lenders, these REITs have a very high sensitivity to interest rate fluctuations and they engage in extensive hedging activity to mitigate interest rate risk. However, like any fixed rate lender, mREITs can be hurt if rates increase (their own borrowing costs increase but their income does not) or hurt if rates drop (mortgage payoffs increase to refinance at lower rates). I find these securities to be quite volatile and do not consider them to be "Sleep Well At Night" investments, so they will not be given further consideration.

A very important fact to keep in mind regarding REITs (and also Master Limited Partnerships) is that these entities do not usually generate enough internal cash flow to pay out their high dividends *and also finance new real estate or fixed asset acquisitions.* This represents a significant difference between REITs and Non-REIT corporations. Since non-REITs are not required to pay such large dividends, they are normally expected to be "self financing," meaning that they should generate enough cash flow to fund capital expenditures *and* pay dividends, without heavy reliance on debt or new equity. As a rule, REITs are not able to do this.

This means that REITs must have ongoing access to both debt and equity capital markets to grow. You will rarely if ever see REITs buying back shares; in fact you will normally see new offerings of stock every few years. This is of course dilutive to existing shareholders, so the expectation is that these new funds will be invested in properties that will produce cash flow accretive to earnings per share. But the inability to be self-funding is a limitation that must always be kept in mind. If the equity and/or debt markets should freeze up, this could have a very serious impact on REIT growth and performance.

Many investors believe that REITs behave like bonds or fixed income products, wherein performance is negative during periods of rising interest rates. But this does not seem to be the case. Throughout the seven periods of rising interest rates since 1972, REIT total return increased in five such periods and declined in two.[12] During the six tightening periods since 1979, REITs produced an average annual total return of 11.4%.[13] During the last period of Federal Reserve rate hikes (2004-2006), when short-term rates increased from 1.00% to 5.25%, REITs produced a 60% total return, compared to the stock market's 20% increase. [14]

Similarly, REITs tend to perform well in periods of inflation. Such periods normally occur when economic growth is strong. Under such conditions, demand for real estate is high, occupancy is high, and tenants are able to absorb – and pay – increases in rent.

---

12   Altegris Advisors LLC,"Interest Rates & REIT Performance" April 2014.

13   Cohen & Steers,"REITs and Rising Rates" July 2014.

14   Forbes," High Interest Rates Won't Sink REITs" 2/27/2015.

A word of caution: Before I became an active investor, I was led to invest in several REITs that were just in the process of formation. *DON'T DO THIS!!* I learned the hard way what a terrible investment this is. In the first place, you obviously have no data or track record to evaluate. Secondly, it may be years before these REITs start paying dividends. Third, these investments are completely illiquid and cannot be sold. Finally, when (if) these REITs do go public (a "liquidity event"), the share price usually plummets as some investors are anxious to recover their principal. I learned the hard way – *avoid any private, non-publically traded REIT* (or any other private company, for that matter!)

You will find the website SeekingAlpha.com is an excellent source to evaluate and learn about REITs. One of the regular contributors, Brad Thomas, writes at least one or two articles every week on REITs. These articles are thorough, well written, and very helpful.

Master Limited Partnerships

A partnership differs from a corporation in several important respects. First, a corporation is a separate legal entity in the eyes of the law, distinct from its shareholders, and may enter into contracts just as individuals do. As a legal "person," most corporations pay income taxes at the corporate level. Also, the shareholders of a corporation are not liable as individuals for the debts/obligations of the corporation.

A partnership, on the other hand, has no separate legal status and pays no income tax. The income of the partnership is divided periodically between the partners depending on their partnership shares, and each partner pays taxes on an individual basis. Importantly, the general partners are all liable, jointly and severally, for the obligations of the partnership.

As the name implies, limited partners have limited liability, like shareholders in a corporation. Limited partners have no management authority, may not vote, and are liable for partnership obligations only to the extent of their investment in the firm. The general partner(s) pay a distribution to the limited partners, representing a return on their investment (similar to a dividend) which is defined in the partnership agreement. Traditional partnerships are private companies that are not publically traded.

A Master Limited Partnership (MLP) is a type of limited partnership that *is* publically traded on an exchange. The MLP therefore combines the tax advantages of a limited partnership (explained below) with the liquidity of a publically traded security. The limited partners provide the capital to the partnership and the general partner manages the MLP's affairs and receives compensation linked to the performance of the entity.

To qualify as an MLP, federal law requires that at least 90% of partnership income must be derived from certain businesses, most of which relate to the use of natural resources. The largest group of MLPs consists of pipeline companies that facilitate the extraction, transportation, storage, refining, and distribution of oil and natural gas. Such MLPs may be referred to as "upstream" (exploration and extraction), "midstream" (transportation and storage), or "downstream" (refining and distribution).

Unlike REITs, MLPs are *not* required by statute to pay out any specific percentage of net income to the partners. However, in practice MLPs do make very high distribution payouts relative to cash flow.[15]

The partnership agreement requires the quarterly (or monthly) distribution of "all available cash" after the general partner establishes a reserve for working capital, debt service, and future distributions.

Given these high payouts, MLPs, like REITs, require ongoing access to capital markets for new equity and debt to fund capital expenditures and growth.

In addition to high payouts and high yields, MLPs also offer investors attractive tax benefits. This occurs because only a small portion of MLP distributions, usually about 20%, is classified and taxed as current income. The majority of the distribution is classified as a *return of capital (ROC)*, and no taxes are assessed on this portion of the distribution until the investment is sold. At that time the total accumulated ROC is taxed (a portion is taxed as capital gains and a portion taxed as ordinary income).[16]

So *taxes are not avoided, rather they are deferred.* Nevertheless, this can be a very attractive benefit if the investment is held for a long period.

While MLPs provide higher yields and attractive tax benefits, they may prove cumbersome when preparing your tax

---

15   Payouts received from MLPs are *distributions*, not dividends.

16   The tax treatment of ROC is explained in **Attachment D**.

returns. Corporations report dividends and capital gains on a 1099 form which is usually summarized in a single report from your brokerage firm. This form is received in late January or early February, in plenty of time to prepare your tax returns. MLPs, however, send out a K-1 form, and you will get a separate K-1 form from each MLP you own. These forms may arrive as late as mid March, and the filing instructions are *far* more complicated than those for 1099 forms. If you use an accountant to prepare your returns, you will save some headaches!

Also note that MLPs are *not appropriate investments for tax sheltered accounts such as an IRA*. If you exceed a certain income level from MLPs, this will trigger a special tax on your IRA earnings. So you should confine MLP ownership to your taxable investment accounts.

Funds: Open End, Closed End, Exchange Traded

Up to this point we have been discussing *individual* securities, which have included common stocks, REITs, and MLPs. We now turn to considering security *funds*. Funds are simply investment pools in which initial investors contribute money into a new entity and receive shares in that entity (fund). The fund then purchases a number of individual securities – possibly as many as a several hundred – which are consistent with the objectives and criteria established by the fund organizer/ sponsor. Fund shareholders receive income and capital gains distributions from the fund (if any), and may sell or redeem their shares – hopefully at a gain – at any time.

The primary advantage of fund investing may be summarized in one word – *diversification.* Instead of investing in individual securities, a fund gives the investor indirect ownership of dozens or hundreds of securities. So if one or even several of these individual companies perform very poorly, the risk is minimized by being spread over a very large population. This means your investment risk is lower than if you owned a small number of individual securities.

The two traditional types of funds are Open-End funds (mutual funds) and Closed-End funds (also known as investment trusts). Another type of fund, the Exchange Traded Fund (ETF), has gained rapidly in popularity over the past twenty years.

Open-End funds are, as the name implies, "open" to new investors, who may invest at any time. These new contributions are invested by the fund and increase the Net Asset Value (NAV) of the fund, and new fund shares are issued to the new investor. Similarly, investors may sell/redeem their shares at any time, and the fund must then sell securities (or reduce cash) to cover these withdrawals, reducing Net Asset Value (NAV). Open-End funds are not traded on an exchange, and all purchases and redemptions actually occur at the end of the trading day after all fund share transactions have been tabulated and all securities repriced. This establishes a new Net Asset Value/share, which is the single price at which all purchases and redemptions for that day are executed.

Closed-End funds (CEFs), again as the name implies, are *not* opened to new investors on any regular basis. The fund is established with initial capital, this capital is invested in a pool of securities, and shares are issued to these original investors. The fund is closed at that point and no new investors may invest and no new shares are issued. These original fund shares are then freely traded on an exchange according to the law of supply and demand. The price of the shares is determined with each trade, not at the end of the day.

This means that there is no direct link between the price of CEF shares and the Net Asset Value (NAV) of the fund. If investors like the fund, demand will exceed supply and the share price may trade at a *premium* to NAV. If investors are less impressed with the fund, supply will exceed demand and the share price may trade at a *discount* to NAV.

This structure creates one advantage for Closed-End funds. If more fund shares are being offered for sale than demand can absorb, the share price will fall. *But the manager of the fund does not have to sell any securities to meet these sales.* The shares are in effect "untethered" from the fund itself; nothing that happens in trading CEF shares has any direct effect on what the fund managers must do. The managers of an Open-End fund must sell securities to meet share redemptions, and such sales may not be in the best interest of the fund if the manager wishes to hold on to these securities. But the CEF manager can ignore fund share transactions and focus strictly on the merits of the securities in his portfolio, selling (and buying) based strictly on portfolio criteria, not fund share buy/sell criteria.

Another advantage to Closed-End funds is *leverage (borrowing)*. CEFs are permitted to borrow money to buy more securities for the fund. Obviously the constraint is that the cost of the borrowed money should be less than the return earned by the securities purchased with this leverage. If this is so, then the leverage can add significantly to the fund's performance. But if interest costs increase and/or portfolio returns decline, leverage can work in the other direction, reducing fund performance.

Another risk of leverage relates to the covenants (restrictions) that a lender might place on a CEF.

For example, the lender might require the fund to maintain a certain ratio between the level of borrowing and the NAV of the fund. If in a rapidly declining market the NAV fell and this ratio was exceeded (too much debt), the fund might be forced to sell securities at depressed prices to reduce debt (similar to a margin call). This could lock in a serious loss that would not be recovered when the market improved, and could permanently impair share value.

The great majority of Open-End funds and CEFs are professionally managed by a senior portfolio manager or managers who are backed up by a team of security analysts. The resumes of these people are usually quite impressive, listing extensive investment experience enhanced by advanced degrees and certifications. Naturally these professionals are paid very well, and to justify their salaries these managers usually set up a specific goal or benchmark return which they try to outperform.

During the great bull market of the '80s and '90s, only an occasional academic study questioned whether these managers were able to consistently achieve the goals they had established. But over the past fifteen years, as investment returns have frequently been dismal or worse, a growing debate has arisen: Are fund managers earning the fees – substantial fees – that they are paid? A growing body of evidence indicates that *the great majority of active portfolio managers do not beat the market and do not achieve their goals on a consistent basis. Therefore management fees are for the most part unjustified.*[17]

As a result, a new group of funds known as Exchange Traded Funds (ETFs) has arisen over the past two decades. Most ETFs are *not* actively managed, but are instead invested to track a specific market index (such as the Standard & Poor's 500 Stock Average) and no attempt is made to out-perform this index. Hence there is no active management and the fees associated with ETFs are very low. The assumption here is that active management is not capable of beating the index, so why pay them to try?

Like CEFs, ETFs trade throughout the day at prices determined by supply and demand, and they are not redeemed once a day at Net Asset Value as Open-End funds are. However, the structure of originating ETFs is such that the trades always remain very close in price to the NAV. So in this sense ETFs combine the best of both Open-End funds and CEFs.

There are now over 7,000 Open-End funds with total assets in excess of $12 trillion. There are over 1500 EFTs with assets of just under $2 trillion. CEFs are *far* smaller in both number and assets under management, with fewer than 600 funds in existence and $250 billion under management.[18]

I have reviewed and analyzed dozens of ETFs and Open-End funds. The basic problem that I have with both types of funds is that *the yields are just too low.* Here are the current (May 2015) yields of several such funds which are specifically dedicated to the generation of dividend income:

---

17   Many references could be cited here. I would recommend *Index Funds* by Mark Hebner, IFA Publishing, 2011.

18   bankrate.com, "Three Fund Types," March 4 2014.

Open End Funds	Exchange Traded Funds
Vanguard Dividend Growth (VDIGX): 1.83%	Schwab US Dividend Equity ETF (SCHD): 2.69%
T Rowe Price Dividend Growth (PRDGX): 1.59%	Vanguard Dividend Appreciation ETF (VIG): 2.14%
Blackrock Equity Dividend (MADVX): 1.83%	ProShares S&P 500 Dividend Aristocrats (NOBL): 1.64%
Columbia Dividend Fund (CDVIX): 2.38%	Vanguard High Dividend Yield ETF (VYM): 2.84%
BNY Mellon Income Stock (MPISX): 2.11%	SPDR S&P Dividend ETF (SDY): 2.25%

I have therefore turned to the Closed End Funds for further consideration and have found a number of CEFs that I find attractive and have invested in. These high yield funds invest in equity securities, including both common and preferred stocks, and also in high yield bonds. Some have a specific industry focus, such as utilities, healthcare, or technology, while others are widely diversified. Some employ leverage while others do not borrow. Some sell at small premiums to NAV, others at a small discount. So I think that the funds I own cover the general gamut of the CEF universe.

Several of these CEF funds have adopted a *Managed Distribution Plan (MDP)*. Such funds have adopted a policy of maintaining the same distribution year after year, regardless of swings in income or capital gains. Consistent distribution is a very strong plus for an income investor, and I note that all my funds with a MDP have accumulated very strong capital reserves, indicating that they have not overpaid, but rather have retained excess cash flow that might have been paid out under a more aggressive approach.

Many investors focus carefully on fund expense ratios and tend to avoid funds where this ratio is high.

I am somewhat out of step on this point. Obviously I would prefer lower expenses, but my real focus is quite simple: *What does this fund pay me?* If the distribution is high enough, I frankly don't care a great deal about how much money the managers are making. As long as the fund balance sheet is strong and the distributions are well covered by fund income, that's good enough for me. If the fund managers can keep it up, I don't mind what the fees are. But, as I say, I think I am in the minority on this point.

I would be careful about CEF liquidity. Most of these funds are not large and many have total assets of $200-$500 million. Trading volume can be thin and if there is a sudden movement in interest rates, price swings can be significant. I have also noticed that CEF prices can be affected toward the end of the year due to income tax motivated selling. Nevertheless, since I am not a trader and not focused on capital gains, I am comfortable with those funds which meet my standards for yield and safety.

Business Development Companies

Business Development Companies (BDCs) are another relatively new asset class, created by Congress in 1980 as a new category of closed-end funds. Like REITs with real estate and MLPs with natural resources, BDCs were created to provide small investors with access to a specialized marketplace – the private equity and venture capital marketplace, previously restricted to very large individual and institutional investors.

BDCs participate in the PE/VC market by making short-term loans to lower-middle and middle market companies. Such companies typically have revenues of between $10-200 million and receive BDC loans ranging from $2-50 million. These loans may be unsecured or secured by first or second liens on assets. Most loans are structured with variable interest rates, reducing exposure to interest rate changes.

BDCs frequently add equity warrants or rights to their loans to enhance the return.

BDCs are required to invest at least 70% of their assets in privately held or thinly traded public companies. In addition, BDCs are required to provide management assistance to their clients and may actually exert significant control over company affairs.

Like REITs, BDCs are required to pay out at least 90% of taxable income to shareholders. In fact most BDCs pay out 98% of taxable income in order to avoid all income taxes. So again like REITs and MLPs, BDCs serve as income tax "pass throughs" wherein the business pays no taxes, which are instead paid by the shareholder. The shareholder tax rate will depend on the breakdown of BDC income – BDC ordinary income will be taxed at ordinary rates and BDC capital gains will be taxed at capital gains rates.

BDCs use shareholder equity and borrowed funds to finance their loans and investments. However, the amount of borrowed money (leverage) may not exceed the amount of equity, so the maximum debt/equity ratio is 1:1, a conservative limit. This is far below the leverage ratio that commercial banks employ, which is normally in excess of 10:1.

As readily marketable, exchange listed securities, BDCs provide investors with access to the high yield private equity marketplace, and they also provide excellent liquidity. As mentioned above, they are technically structured as closed-end funds, and as such their investments are spread over virtually all industry categories. So BDCs provide broad sector diversification to dozens of companies, whereas traditional PE/VC investments involved large, illiquid commitments to individual private concerns.

The BDC marketplace remained relatively quiet until 2000 when the formation of new BDCs accelerated. As of October 2014 there were 51 BDC companies with a combined market value of $35 billion. This is quite small when viewed against the market cap of $263 billion for traditional closed-end funds.[19]

I think of BDCs as a cross between a traditional closed-end fund and a commercial bank. I analyze BDCs as I do all closed-end funds, and we will discuss this analysis protocol in detail in Section Four. But as BDC loans are usually short term and variable rate, they are similar to traditional banks loans more so than bonds. In that regard I like to look at the percentage of loans on non-accrual, just as I would if analyzing a bank. I would be concerned to find the level of non-accruals increasing rapidly and/or in excess of 1-2%.

---

19 The ABCs of Business Development Companies," Forbes, December 1, 2014.

High Yield Bonds

OK, I might as well get this over with. Yes, I am now going to write about *junk bonds*. Some of you may already be turning the page, but if you will bear with me for a few moments, I would like to introduce an asset class that I think may be an appropriate addition to a diversified portfolio.

First of all, a quick definition: The term "high yield" applies to any debt security that does not carry an investment grade credit rating. Standard and Poor's investment grade ratings range from AAA all the way down to BBB-, considered the lowest investment grade. Therefore, high yield bond (HYB) ratings would range from a high of BB+, through BB, BB-, B+, B, B-, CCC, CC, C and D (in default). I would also include bonds that have no credit rating at all, as would be the case for smaller, private companies.

High yield bonds (HYB) have always been with us, but if you go back forty years or so, they were then known as "fallen angels" – bonds initially issued as investment grade securities that had deteriorated in credit quality and were therefore selling at substantial discounts to par value. This was a small, specialized, higher-risk market that received virtually no attention from individual investors.

All this changed in 1977 when Michael Milken, a bond trader at Drexel Burnham Lambert, convinced his firm to underwrite bonds for smaller, unproven companies that were considered *speculative from the start*. Such underwriting, which provided speed in accessing capital as well as fixed rate financing, exploded in the 1980's when numerous firms became involved in hostile takeovers. Since Drexel and other investment firms now made a broad secondary market for such securities, the liquidity thus provided enabled smaller investors to enter the HYB market.

Unfortunately, Mr. Milken and certain other bond financiers were ultimately indicted for securities fraud and went to prison. This scandal was widely reported and to this day the details continue to tarnish not only the reputation of the individuals and investment firms involved (Drexel went bankrupt), but also the credibility of the companies that raise capital through the HYB market. To some investors, this old scandal – and the continuing use of the term "junk bonds" – leaves the impression that high-yield borrowers are somehow "shady" and are simply unattractive per se. This is indeed a shame, and certainly unwarranted.

Over the past 35 years the high yield bond market has been used by hundreds of medium-sized, growing companies that are too young, too small, or too undercapitalized to receive an investment grade rating. Virtually all industries have actively participated in the HYB market, including media and entertainment, healthcare, telecommunications, technology, utilities, energy, autos, and consumer products. The total global market for high yield debt is now estimated by Morgan Stanley at $2 trillion, compared to $4.2 trillion in outstanding investment grade debt. Therefore, HYB represents approximately one third (32%) of all outstanding debt issues.

As the name obviously implies, the primary advantage of HYB securities is a high level of current income. Because HYB borrowers lack an investment grade rating – and therefore involve more risk – these firms must offer a higher interest rate to compensate for this higher level of risk. In general, HYB securities yield about 400 - 500 basis points (4-5%) above the yield for US Treasury securities, although this spread may by slightly lower when HYB securities are in strong demand, or substantially higher when investors fear a weak economy, credit deterioration, and/or a higher default level.

An investor can purchase individual bonds, just as one can purchase individual stocks. However, there are three reasons why I don't do this. First, there is a considerable amount of analysis that must be done and the protocol for bond analysis is significantly different from stock or fund analysis. Second, the risk of default is always there, which would produce a very drastic reduction in principal value. Third, the market for individual bonds is not as liquid as the market for common stocks, so price swings can be more pronounced.

I prefer to invest in HYB securities through closed end funds. First, these funds are actively managed by professional financial analysts who can – I hope! – do the thorough analysis necessary to construct a sound portfolio. Second, these funds own hundreds of individual bonds across a broad spectrum of industries, so I achieve full diversification. Third, the trading liquidity of a multi-million or billion dollar NYSE bond fund is certainly higher than that of a small holding of individual bonds. Fourth, CEFs can use leverage of up to roughly 30% of total assets, enhancing yield significantly – 9-10% distribution rates are relatively easy to obtain here.

There are two basic areas of risk that HYB investors need to be aware of:

- **Interest Rate Risk**

Every fixed rate security (bond/note) is exposed to the risk of a change in interest rates. The market value of any bond changes inversely with a change in interest rates. So if interest rates rise, bond prices will fall, while a decrease in rates will cause bond prices to rise.

HYBs are in fact _less_ sensitive to interest rate changes than high grade bonds. This may at first seem counterintuitive, as investment grade bonds are higher in quality/lower in risk. However, HYBs have shorter maturities (usually 5-7 years) than investment grade bonds, which may be issued with maturities up to 30 years. The longer the maturity, the longer the bond is exposed to the affect of an interest rate change, hence the greater the price adjustment necessary to reflect the new yield. Secondly, HYBs carry significantly higher coupon rates, so that a given change in external interest rates requires less change in price to achieve an adjusted yield. So HYBs actually have an advantage over investment grade bonds in terms of interest rate exposure.[20]

The easiest way to gauge a bond's sensitivity to interest rate changes is to look at the *duration* of the bond. The duration of a bond (or bond fund) is the average time (years) it takes to collect all the contractual interest and principal payments due on the bond or bonds. The duration will almost always be shorter than the maturity, since all bonds (except zero coupon bonds) pay interest monthly or quarterly, thereby reducing the total collection time below the maturity date. If periodic principal payments are also required, the duration is further reduced.

As you might expect, the shorter the duration, the lower the sensitivity to interest rate changes. Most high yield bond funds have durations between 3.5–5 years. As the current expectation is for interest rates to increase, I would generally try to keep bond duration at lower levels.

- **Default Risk**

There is no question that the risk of default is higher with HYBs than with investment grade bonds. But the real question is: Does the higher interest rate (reward) compensate adequately for the higher risk? Secondly, since most HYBs are secured by fixed assets and/or carry a high priority in bankruptcy liquidation, what is the recovery rate if a bond defaults?

Regarding the first question, a study performed on "fallen angels" many years ago showed that the extra yield offered by

---

20   See **Attachment E** for a more detailed discussion of interest rate risk.

HYBs *more than compensated for the risk of default*. In fact it was this study that Michael Milken read as an undergraduate that led him to specialize in HYBs. I am not aware of any update on this study, but one could make the general observation that if the average default rate on HYBs is around 4% per year and the median yield spread over treasuries is 5.6%,[21] then an investor should expect a positive long run result. However, that conclusion is *much* less certain in the short run, as yield spread and default rate are very volatile and rarely converge to "normal" at the same time.

Regarding the question of recovery rate, the average recovery in a HYB default is approximately 40%.[22]

So it is important to realize that even in the event of default, the ultimate value of a HYB does not fall to zero. Therefore it would appear that we should adjust our default rate from 4% to an effective "true loss" rate of perhaps 2.4%. So this would bolster the real positive spread over US Treasury securities.

HYBs tend to be correlated much more closely with equities than with high grade bonds. HYBs tend to perform well when default rates are low, which is usually the case when the economy is strong and corporate cash flow is predictable. This of course is the normal scenario when stocks are also performing well. So it would not be appropriate to think of HYBs as a means of diversifying an equity portfolio, as the two assets classes tend to move in tandem rather than in opposition.

Interest earned on individual bonds is taxed as ordinary income. However, distributions from HYB closed-end funds may contain some amount of realized capital gains or return on capital, which receive preferential tax treatment.

---

21   "Distribution of High Yield Spreads," Hotchkis & Wiley, 2012.

22   "Defaults and Returns in the High Yield Bond Market," New York University School of business, 2011.

Municipal Bonds

Municipal bonds are debt obligations, both long- and short-term, issued by any US government body or agency at or below the state level. They are used to finance virtually any type of public facility, including schools, toll roads, bridges, utilities, airports, hospitals, and subsidized housing, or used for general operating expenses. These bonds may be general (unsecured) obligations of the issuer or secured by specified project revenues.

The primary advantage of municipal bonds to the investor is that in almost all cases the interest paid is exempt from federal taxation. If the bonds are issued by a government body in the state where the investor resides, interest may also be exempt from state and/or local income taxes as well.

Due to their tax-advantaged status, municipal bond interest rates are lower than rates on taxable debt. The higher one's personal tax rate, the more attractive the after-tax yield on municipal bonds will be.

As an example, assume an investor's tax rate is 25%. If the yield on a taxable corporate bond is 4.0%, the effective after-tax yield would be 4.0% X (1 - .25) = 3.0%. Therefore, any municipal bond offering a tax-exempt rate higher than 3.0% would be attractive. If the investor's tax rate is 35%, any municipal bond offering a rate higher than 4.0% X (1 - .35) = 2.6% would be attractive.

Municipal bonds are rated for credit soundness by all three of the primary credit rating agencies (Moody's, Standard & Poor's, and Fitch). Municipal bonds have historically shown very low default rates compared to corporate issues. There are thousands of municipal bonds that carry solid investment grade ratings and certainly no need to invest in any municipal security with a rating less than BBB.

Municipal bonds tend to have longer average maturities – and therefore longer durations – so sensitivity to interest rate changes is high. Individual participation in this market is quite high, and many investors hold these securities until maturity.

As with high yield bonds, I prefer to hold municipal bonds through closed-end funds established for this asset class. This achieves good geographic diversification and, with leverage, after-tax yields of 6%.

Summary: Section Two

Investors seeking solid income and income growth may now choose from a number of attractive alternatives. In addition to the traditional equity investments of common and preferred stock, there are now three relatively new asset classes that were not available two generations ago. These new investment categories include real estate investment trusts, master limited partnerships, and business development companies. These securities offer individual investors access to markets that were formerly the domain of very wealthy or institutional investors who could commit large sums for an extended (illiquid) period of time. These new securities offer high yields, solid distribution growth, virtually instant liquidity, and avoid the problem of double corporate taxation.

Investors may choose to buy individual securities, or they may prefer to invest in funds, including open-end (mutual) funds, closed-end funds, or ETFs (Exchange Traded Funds). Funds provide broad diversification across industry sectors, geography, cyclicality, asset classes, or market capitalization.

Open- and closed-end funds are managed by financial professionals, and there is considerable debate as to the level and value of the fees they charge. ETFs are generally not managed, charge much lower fees, and track a specific market index with no attempt to out-perform the market.

Given the relatively low yields available in open-end funds and ETFs, I prefer to invest in closed-end funds for positions in high yield and municipal bonds, as well as stocks. Closed-end funds provide diversification, but in addition may provide leverage to boost returns. There is always some additional risk with borrowing, and in addition CEFs represent a much smaller market where liquidity can be an issue.

Municipal and high yield bonds normally carry fixed rates of interest. Since these interest payments do not increase, this is a negative factor for Dividend Growth Investors. However, the absolute after-tax yields are often high enough so that these securities can represent an attractive addition to a diversified portfolio.

I do not invest in US Government or investment grade bonds. This decision runs counter to the advice offered by most investment professionals, who maintain that bonds offer important diversification strengths to counterbalance equity value fluctuations. This may indeed be so, but with high grade bond yields at current miniscule levels, buying such bonds would clearly sacrifice significant income, perhaps too much income to achieve the primary goal of a 100% organic income portfolio.

SECTION THREE

HOW:
Corporations and Partnerships

"All of us who have been saving over our working years have been trained to believe that capital appreciation over time is what it is all about. It takes a disciplined mind to adjust that thinking when it comes time to replace capital appreciation with long term reliable income. There are those that can do this, and there are those who cannot."

— *Bruce Miller, Seeking Alpha.com contributor, May 7, 2015*

What This Section Will Cover

In order to construct a quality Dividend Growth Portfolio that is strong, consistent, and balanced, an investor should adopt a rigorous protocol that will be consistently applied to evaluate both the essential *qualitative* characteristics as well as the *quantitative* metrics of each security under consideration.

- **Qualitative**
  1. We need a good understanding of the products and/or services offered and the present and projected demand for these goods and services – what is the expected product life cycle?
  2. We should understand the broad social, technological, economic and geopolitical trends affecting this particular industry.
  3. We need to focus particular attention on the company's economic "moat" – the sustainable competitive advantages (or lack thereof) that it enjoys over its competitors.
  4. We should evaluate management's ability to achieve financial goals and allocate capital effectively according to sound strategic planning.

- **Quantitative**

  The bulk of this section will focus on the construction of a quantitative model that may be applied to evaluate and rank corporations and partnerships for purchase. This model measures and evaluates the metrics of a single business entity. In the following section, we will develop a model that will evaluate open-end, closed-end, and exchange traded funds. The metrics employed by these two models are somewhat different, since it is not possible to know individual performance data for each of the hundreds of companies held within a fund.

Our model will address these three specific questions:

- What metrics should be considered in evaluating a dividend growth stock?
- Of the metrics selected, what relative importance (weight) should be assigned to each metric?
- How can the weighted metrics then be evaluated within a single, unified model?

We select ten performance metrics within the following three categories and weight them as follows:

- Dividend Yield and Growth: 40%
- Dividend Protection: 44%
- Market Performance: 16%

In order to screen stocks for portfolio selection, we will begin with a *Preliminary Review* which will eliminate the great majority of stocks from further consideration. Those that pass the Preliminary Review are subjected to a comprehensive *Final Review* of the metrics listed above, where a final score (maximum of 1000) will be determined. This final score may then be used to rank stocks as purchase candidates.

We will end this section with a general discussion of diversification of securities by asset class and by industry to insure a balanced portfolio.

Qualitative Considerations

Product/Service

It is just basic common sense that we need to have a solid understanding of the products and/or services offered by a company and the uses or purposes which these products serve. We should feel comfortable that the present and future demand for these products appears strong. We should be aware of the broad social, technological, economic, and geopolitical forces at play that affect demand – and therefore pricing and profits – in the future.

Virtually every company will encounter occasional – perhaps even predictable – cyclical or seasonal downturns. This might be of considerable concern to a stock trader looking for a quick profit, but of minor concern to a long term Dividend Growth Investor. But what happens if the product begins to experience a more prolonged downward trend?

So many examples come to mind here. Who could have imagined in the 1950s that American automobiles, steel, and manufacturing in general were about to enter a period of profound long-term decline? Or that millions of Americans would give up smoking within a generation? That Middle Eastern oil producers would form OPEC and drive oil prices over $100/barrel? That computers would become cost efficient for home and personal use? That banks would move beyond state boundaries to form nationwide financial monoliths? The list is endless.

In addition to such broad and dramatic developments, there are smaller, more subtle changes that can sneak up on a company and suddenly burst to the surface. Let me relate two recent and rather painful examples that occurred in my own portfolio:

Two years ago I purchased shares in Century Link, the third

largest telecommunications company in the United States (although it is *far* smaller than AT&T and Verizon, the two largest telecoms). I read the report of an online analyst that was rather tepid, noting that the *consumer land line business was shrinking. Cable and wireless were taking this business away*, and Century Link had no significant presence in these markets. Nevertheless, the score of my model was fairly strong and dividend coverage was solid. So I went ahead.

Less than a month after my purchase, Century Link cut its dividend by 25%, and the stock price also dropped 25% -- overnight! This action took the street completely by surprise, but the directors had come to the conclusion that significant capital investment was required and that future cash flows would not sustain the dividend. I held on and the stock price recovered somewhat and I eventually sold at a small loss. Since then the company's sales have remained stagnant and the share price has continued to fall.

On another occasion I purchased shares in Mattel Inc., the world's largest toy manufacturer. Again I reviewed the online analysis and noted one disquieting fact: Mattel relied on its traditional lines (Barbie, Fisher Price, American Girl) but it *was not participating actively in the market for electronic and digital toys and games*. The basic underlying trend is that *children are now aging out of traditional toys quicker*. Toys that once appealed to a 12-year old were now of little interest to any child older than 9 or 10. But the numbers looked very good, dividend coverage was strong, and so I bought in.

Mattel's stock price rose nicely for almost a year, but then leading lines like Barbie began to show revenue declines. As sales stagnated – and then fell – operating margins dropped significantly and dividend coverage evaporated. Given my temporary capital gain, I held on as the stock price fell – too long as it turned out – and eventually sold at a small loss.

In both cases – both Century Link and Mattel – I chose to

ignore clear information that new demographic trends were at work. *Consumer preferences were changing in fundamental ways, and these two companies were not well equipped to cope with these changes.* These were not temporary cyclical swings – these were not random variances – these were more profound behavioral shifts. I ignored them at my peril.

Such pitfalls seem obvious in hindsight, but they are perhaps not so obvious when you first read about them. For example, sales of carbonated beverages are declining at Coca Cola, the traditional mainstay of the company. Same-store sales at McDonald's are down, and competition is intense. This would give me pause if I were considering buying these stocks, but what if I already owned them – as I do? Should I sell, or give management a chance to overcome these challenges?

McDonald's is older than I am, and Coca Cola is twice as old as I am. Together they have increased their dividends for 90 consecutive years. They have perhaps the two strongest brands in any business or industry in the world. Both balance sheets are strong, although the payout ratios have increased.

I'm sticking with both – for now. We shall see whether management can rise to the occasion, or whether I'll kick myself some day for ignoring the writing on the wall......

A related issue to consider is product life cycle. Certain products have very long life cycles – you can expect such products to be around for one or more lifetimes. Most consumer staples – flour, soap, toothpaste, bathroom tissue – are examples here, as would be energy (oil, gas) and utility power generation. Yet even here there can and will be long term trends at work, such as the introduction of generic consumer products or alternative energy sources. Pharmaceutical companies enjoy patent protection for their drug products, but this protection will disappear within a generation. And at the other extreme, consider electronic devices, which are now virtually obsolete by the time they come to market. Consider the fortunes of BlackBerry or Nokia and I think you – like me – might be reluctant to invest in manufacturers of such devices.

Economic Moat

There are very few true monopolies around today, and virtually every company faces some level of competition. What investors seek are companies that have developed a *sustainable competitive advantage* that can protect and buffer them from the actions of other participants in their industry.

Warren Buffett coined the term "economic moat" to reflect the competitive strength of a company. The image is that of a castle with a moat around it for protection – the wider the better. Wide moat companies have demonstrated their "staying power" – they are dominant in their industry and marketplace. They can meet and beat the competition. They can generate consistent excess returns over their cost of capital that weaker competitors cannot match, due to:

- Buying and pricing power through sheer size
- Product innovation, superiority and differentiation
- Patent protection
- Financial, regulatory, or geographic barriers to competitive entry
- Brand strength and loyalty
- Streamlined and efficient cost structure
- High customer switching costs

Morningstar.com is a premier financial website that establishes an economic moat rating for each of the approximately 1500 stocks that it reviews. The moat ratings assigned – Wide, Narrow, and None – are self-explanatory, again given the visual image of castle with the most protection offered by a wide moat. I will write more about financial websites in a few pages, but I will mention at this point that all of my portfolio holdings have either a wide or a narrow moat. That is part of my Preliminary Screen, and it is one requirement of the screen that I do not compromise.

Another example might be helpful here. Last year I bought the stock of a producer of nitrogen fertilizer with a great track record. But this is strictly a commodity product, essentially identical to the product of any other fertilizer producer, and when nitrogen prices fell sharply, so did the dividend and the price of the stock. The simple fact that I ignored was that *the company had no economic moat*. There was nothing unique – or unique enough – about the company or its product to protect it from competitive pricing pressure. Without an economic moat – without some *sustainable competitive advantage* – I never should have considered the stock for purchase in the first place.

Assessing Management

It is advisable to judge the efficacy of management by considering the following:

- On a per share basis, what is the track record of the company in terms of:
      Sales
      Earnings
      Cash Flow
      Dividends
- Is management effective in allocating capital (investing/directing company assets productively)?
- Is management "shareholder-friendly"?
- How much of the corporation's stock is owned by management "insiders"?
- What are the strategic and tactical goals of the company over the next five years?
- Is management pay – cash and stock – reasonable for a

company of this size in this industry?

To answer these questions, I would recommend the Stock Analysis provided by Morningstar's premium service for any particular company. There is a special section in the report that deals with management, and I like the emphasis the analysts put on allocation of capital. You will get a good sense as to how well management is directing the resources of the company, and whether capital expenditures/acquisitions/ mergers are in the best interest of shareholders. Management stewardship is graded as "exemplary," "standard," or "poor." I would not consider any company with a "poor" management rating.

Customer/Supplier Concentration

Risk is increased whenever revenues and/or inventory purchases are concentrated within a relatively small number of accounts. This factor is particularly relevant within small/micro companies. An attractive history of revenue growth can deteriorate quickly if a major account is lost or even declines.

Similarly, margins can be dramatically reduced and/or working capital stretched if a major supplier changes price or payment terms. I would be careful in evaluating any company wherein one customer is responsible for more than 20% of total revenues, or one supplier is responsible for more than 30% of total purchases. You will have to review the regulatory filings carefully to find such information.

Client concentration is an important factor with REITs. You will want to see broad tenant diversification in terms of numbers, square footage, type of property, and geography. You will also want to see that leases expire over an extended period and are not concentrated within the next few years.

Macro Economic Considerations

Any conscientious investor needs to know what is going on in the economy at large and what broad trends are at work that may influence economic growth and security prices. Projected trends in gross domestic product, interest rates, inflation, unemployment, Federal Reserve policy, budget deficits, and international financial and political developments are all ongoing metrics that every investor needs to understand and follow. Similarly, sudden exogenous shocks, such as a collapse in oil prices, sweeping regulatory changes, or a market liquidity crunch, should be monitored as well.

Having said this, I am at the same time reluctant to place too much emphasis on macro economic forecasts as the basis for stock selection and timing. I say this for the simple reason that economic forecasts can be wrong – in fact, way wrong. For example, at the beginning of 2014, virtually every economist predicted that interest rates would rise. They didn't. They continued to decline. And if you had sold off your bonds, you would have been sorely disappointed. As the Federal Reserve increased the money supply dramatically over the past few years, many pundits warned about raging inflation and a decline in the dollar. Neither happened – so if you had rushed out to buy gold in 2012, you would not be a happy camper today. We have been told for the past three years that a major correction in stock prices was "immanent," yet as of this writing, the market still holds on to its gains.

There is a tremendous amount of "noise" in the investment world. There are alarmists shouting at us all the time, trying to create headlines that will justify their existence and opinions. It takes time to figure out who is worth listening to, what web sites to visit, and which newsletters are nuanced and insightful. I think the sources of information that I will identify in this book are professional, balanced, fair, and well worth the "price of admission." I think they will serve you well.

A Dividend Growth Investor is a long term investor. I try to interpret financial news by taking a long term perspective: Does this event follow a cyclical pattern – *have we seen this before* – or is this a unique new development that deserves more research and investigation? That is why I am not overly concerned with the recent drop in the price of oil – this has happened before. It may take a year or two for supply and demand to readjust to normal levels, but I believe that it will happen. Similarly, I am not concerned if interest rates rise, because I have lived through the interest rate cycle several times during my adult life. So if I own Chevron, I will continue to hold it as it has proven to me that it is a resilient, quality company. If I own the REIT Realty Income Corporation, I will continue to hold that as well. The fundamentals are still sound, even if the company is temporarily out of favor with "Mr. Market."

Quantitative Considerations

Introduction

I have read numerous investment guides and manuals over the past few years on the subject of stock selection. In addition to the qualitative factors that we have already discussed, these sources give the reader an extensive list of quantitative metrics to "consider" – a host of financial ratios, growth trends and forecasts, performance history, industry comparables, analyst rankings, credit ratings, and so forth. While all of these metrics are indeed important to consider, the reader is left with no real sense as to:

- How does the investor narrow this broad list of metrics down to a manageable number?
- Of the metrics selected, which are the most important? What weights do we apply to each?
- How does one evaluate these weighted metrics within a single, unified model to determine which stock is preferable to which other stock?

Without a comprehensive, quantitative system to evaluate stocks, it is extremely difficult to approach stock selection in a consistent manner. If you pick stocks through random, unstructured judgments, including some metrics while ignoring others, then you are going to wind up with a hodge-podge of securities that have no unifying, common characteristics. I know from my own experience how easy it is to pick a stock because it has one or two very attractive attributes, while ignoring more negative characteristics. So I think it is critical *to develop a protocol – a rigorous discipline in which every stock is subjected to extensive tests that measure all aspects of corporate strength.*

And I want this *protocol to be as quantitative as possible.* Certain qualitative judgments must be made, as we have just discussed. But to the extent that we can reduce our testing to numeric calculations, that eliminates subjective or emotional considerations from the process.

Another point to consider is the extent to which we rely on *future estimates as opposed to past performance*. I am going to come down hard on the side of past performance. Certainly investment theory tells us that we want to look to the future and make the best projections we can as to where this company will be in five or ten years. But in order to do this, we must begin with a projection of future earnings. How do we do this? Well, shouldn't we turn to the experts, the CFAs, who do this for a living?

As I write this, here are estimates of future earnings growth (5 years) for the following companies:

	CLOROX	COCA COLA	AT&T	CHEVRON
Investing website #1:	6.6%	5.2%	4.7%	-8.2%
Investing website #2:	8.7%	9.1%	-1.2%	3.1%
Investing website #3:	7.0%	4.9%	4.7%	-1.7%
Investing website #4:	8.5%	6.0%	7.0%	2.5%

Remember that these are NOT start-up companies but established, mature dividend aristocrats.

Yet the experts – with the possible exception of Clorox – are dramatically dispersed in their estimates. So if the experts are so divergent, *what are we supposed to do?*

So I will propose a comprehensive, quantitative protocol to evaluate dividend stocks. This protocol consists of ten metrics based on past performance that I believe will test all the fundamental elements of corporate strength.

"We have two classes of forecasters:
those who don't know – and those who don't
know that they don't know."

— John Kenneth Galbraith, Economist

"The future is inherently unknown and unknowable.
Those who claim otherwise
are trying to sell you something"

-- Barry Ritholtz, columnist, Washington Post, June 26, 2016

Metrics for Analyzing Dividend Growth Stocks

Presented below are the ten metrics we will use to evaluate DGI stocks and other securities:

I. Dividend Yield and Growth

Current Dividend Yield

Definition: Projected dividend dollar amount over the next twelve months ÷ Current stock price

Comment: This is the most important metric we will consider. This is the bottom line. This tells us the percentage income return we expect to receive on our investment. Please note that the calculation begins with the most recent periodic dividend (assume quarterly), annualized (multiplied by 4), divided by price. This is the *projected yield for the next twelve months,* not the yield for the past year.

Five Year Projected Dividend Yield

Definition: Current Dividend Yield compounded[23] over five years by a selected growth rate

Comment: The second word of our DGI strategy is *growth.* We expect our dividends to increase every year, providing a compound growth stimulus to our portfolio. We insist on a minimum growth rate (2%) that will be at least equal the rate of inflation. The selected growth rate is determined by reviewing:

- Percentage gain of the most recent year-over-year dividend increase
- Weighted average dividend growth rate (WAGR) over the past five years[23]
- Dividend growth rates projected by investment advisory firms (IE: Value Line, Morningstar)

---

23   See **Attachment C** for a discussion of Compound and Weighted Average Growth Rates.

Additional Yield – Share Buybacks

Definition: Compound growth rate (negative) in the reduction of shares outstanding – last three years

Comment: Many companies increase earnings per share (EPS) by buying back their own stock. By reducing the number of shares outstanding, this obviously increases the EPS calculation. All else being equal, a higher EPS should translate to a higher stock price, but this assumes a stable or increasing price/earnings ratio, which is a big assumption. Share buybacks also provide more dividend dollars available to fewer shareholders. So I treat share buybacks as a plus for shareholders, but I give it a lower weight than direct dividend cash payments.[24]

II. Dividend Protection

Dividend Payout Ratio[25]

Definition: Three Year Weighted (3-2-1) Average: Dividends per share ÷ Earnings per share

Comment: Earnings are the ultimate source of dividend payments. The lower the Dividend Payout Ratio, the lower the percentage of earnings that must be allocated to the dividend. Thus a low payout ratio means a "safer" dividend, because there is a greater cushion or a greater degree of protection for the dividend if earnings should decline. Dividend protection is extremely important in my screen and receives a very high weight.[26]

---

24   It is important to focus on the actual reduction in the number of shares and NOT on the amount spent to buy back shares. At times some companies have spent money to buy back shares, only to reissue such shares as employee stock options at a greatly reduced price. This does nothing for other shareholders, and in fact is dilutive to other shareholders.

25   Dividend coverage for real estate investment trusts and master limited partnerships requires another approach and involves special calculations which are presented in **Attachments F and G.**

26   Technically dividends are paid out of cash flow, not earnings. As presented

Balance Sheet

Definition: The balance sheet is a snapshot of the financial position of a company at a particular moment in time. The simplest way to think about a balance sheet is that it shows all the assets the company owns on one page, and then who paid for those assets on the other page. The parties that paid for the assets include: 1) lenders, suppliers, and other creditors (these are grouped as "liabilities") and 2) the shareholders who bought stock in the company (shown as "net worth" or "shareholders' equity." The lower the level of liabilities relative to net worth, the stronger the company.

Comment: We will consider three "sub metrics" when evaluating balance sheet strength:

- Standard & Poor's Credit Rating. These ratings range from AAA to BBB- for "investment grade" companies. Ratings below BBB- are considered less credit worthy. For common stocks we look for an investment grade rating.
- Debt/EBITDA. This ratio measures total debt to the cash flow available to service (repay) that debt. Cash flow (EBITDA) is defined as Earnings Before deductions for Interest, Taxes, Depreciation, and Amortization. A lower (stronger) ratio shows more cash to repay debt.
- Debt/Total Capital. Total capital consists of debt plus shareholder equity. This is a basic ratio of financial strength. The lower (stronger) the ratio, the more the company is financed by its owners (shareholders) rather than its creditors (debt holders).

---

in financial statements, net income (earnings) includes a number of non-cash expenses, such as depreciation. Cash flow, however, is not affected by depreciation, which is simply an accounting entry that involves no cash outlay. Therefore some investors prefer to measure dividend protection by comparing dividends to "free cash flow." See a discussion on this topic in **Attachment H** in the appendix.

Five Year Weighted Average Growth Rate of Cash Flow from Operations (CFO)

Definition: Weighted Average Growth Rate, with weights (5-4-3-2-1) to emphasize most recent years.

Comment: Cash Flow from Operations (CFO) is in my opinion the single most important metric to measure corporate growth. Sales growth can be affected by mergers, acquisitions, divestitures, or discontinued operations, all of which may mask the organic sales growth of the basic book of business. Earnings growth is certainly important, but dividends – our point of focus – are technically not paid from earnings – they are paid from cash flow. CFO shows us just how much net cash the company created through the sale of its products or services. CFO begins with net income, adjusts for all non-cash expenses or deferred items, and includes all balance sheet working capital adjustments. *This metric is the ultimate source of dividend payments, dividend growth, and dividend protection.*

Years of Consecutive Dividend Increases

Definition: Self Explanatory.

Comment: This is the single best metric I know to measure the level of corporate management's commitment to its shareholders. If a company like Coca Cola or Emerson Electric shows you that they have increased their dividend payment every single year for over fifty years, I really don't think you need to know much more about their determination to protect their dividend payout. I do make a slight concession here and will consider the record of increases intact if a company held its dividend steady for two consecutive years (no more) during the recession in 2008 or 2009.

III. Stock Performance

3 – 5 – 10 Year Weighted Average Total Return

Definition: Total Return earned on a stock is the sum of all dividends received plus price appreciation generated within a given period of time.

Comment: We will average the total return for a stock for the periods of three years, five years, and ten years. We apply weights of 3, 2, and 1 respectively to the returns for 10 years, 5 years, and 3 years. We apply the highest weight to the longest period, recognizing that it is more difficult to sustain any given return over a longer period of time.

Ten year Total Return Standard Deviation

Definition: Standard Deviation measures the variability of sample values around the mean (average) of that sample. We calculate the STDEV of all ten total return values for each of the past ten years.

Comment: A lower standard deviation means that the sample values cluster more closely around the mean, and that investors should therefore expect less volatility. There is some argument as to whether volatility per se is synonymous with the concept of risk. But whatever the definition of risk may be, every investor would prefer that his portfolio behave in a stable, steady, non-volatile fashion.

Recession Recovery Index

Definition: ½ X (Maximum recession stock price decline) X (Months to recover to pre-recession high)

Comment: OK, this is my creation, so some explanation is in order.

As a DGI investor, I do not focus primarily on historical or anticipated stock price performance. However, I am certainly interested in this metric, as any investor would be. In particular, as a defensive investor who looks for low volatility, I am very interested to see how a stock performed in the recession of 2008-9. Virtually every stock took a substantial hit between 2007 and 2009. The question therefore is: How big was the hit, and how long did it take to recover to the pre-recession high price?

If you look at the price chart for almost any stock during this period, you will see an "inverted triangle" pattern. The price dives down during 2007-2008, hits a low point in early 2009, and then begins to rebound. Most stocks (but not all) eventually recover to their pre-recession high price. So you have a triangle with a base (on top, actually) measured by the months between pre-recession high price to high price recovery, and a height measured by the percentage of 2007(high)-2009(low) price decline. The area of this triangle measures the degree of "hurt" that stock caused investors. The deeper the plunge, and/or the longer the recovery period, the more pronounced/prolonged was the loss for the investor.

So good old high school trigonometry gives us the answer to the area of the triangle: ½ A B. Hence, the definition listed above. Obviously, the smaller the area, the more limited was the loss experience.

Summary

These then are the ten primary metrics that we will use to build our stock evaluation model. But I want to make a very basic point here. These are – obviously – *my* metrics. I have selected them after thinking for a long time about all the various statistics that investors consider when evaluating a stock. I wanted to construct a model that would satisfy or compromise two conflicting goals: Build a model that is reasonably easy to use, but at the same time comprehensive enough to consider the most basic and important elements of corporate strength. The point I want to make here is that *you may want to design a different model*. Once I take you through the mechanics of model construction and you see how I do it, you may want to re-think the ten metrics I have selected – as well as the weights I have assigned to them – and come up with a model that suits your own perceptions or attitudes about risk and reward. The most important thing is that you will have a model – a protocol – whether it is my model or one of your own design – that you will use in a rigorous and disciplined fashion to evaluate stocks in a consistent manner.

Sources of Investment Data and Guidance

Before we get into the techniques and procedures – the protocol – involved in evaluating stocks, let's take a quick detour at this point to discuss data collection. Everything we do from this point on will require data. Lots and lots of data, to be frank. The nitty-gritty of security analysis involves good old-fashioned number crunching – there's just no way around that. This is not glamorous, but it can be exciting – I hope – because you are involved in a treasure hunt and all this data will lead you to build a solid, balanced portfolio that produces consistent income.

The really good news here is that data collection is far easier and efficient than it was during my banking career in the 1970's, 80's and 90's. The internet now hosts numerous investment sites that present a great amount of free information, including stock price and dividend data, performance history, credit and bond ratings, financial statement spread sheets, financial ratios, and other information. In addition, these sites also offer, for a fee, in-depth security analysis by professional Certified Financial Analysts. DISCLOSURE: I HAVE NO INTEREST – FINANCIAL OR OTHERWISE – IN THE FOLLOWING DATA SOURCES.

- **Morningstar.com**

Morningstar is in my opinion the best web site for financial data and analysis. The site offers a great deal of free information, and with only a few minor exceptions you will be able to obtain everything you need in terms of data collection. You can also set up virtual portfolios on this site and receive minute-to-minute price and value updates, periodic profit and loss results, and diversification and performance feedback.

I strongly recommend that you consider paying for Premium membership. This will give you access to analytical reports on well over 1500 securities, which are prepared by Morningstar's extensive team of Certified Financial Analysts. This is top grade, totally professional work. Each report will give you an extensive summary of the products/services offered, current sales and earnings trends, capital allocation decisions, competitive strengths and industry developments, management stewardship, risks, and current "intrinsic value." This last metric involves a complex present value analysis of projected cash flows under various assumptions, and gives an estimate as to the fair intrinsic value of company's stock today. By comparing this intrinsic fair value to the current market price, this helps to determine *when* to buy, after you have determined *what* to buy.

Another great strength of Morningstar is Josh Peters, who is in charge of dividend investing (although his title is much fancier than that). Josh authors the Dividend Investor newsletter, which tracks a live portfolio of dividend growth stocks. His analysis is very straightforward and extremely helpful. I would also recommend subscribing to his newsletter, which is published monthly with weekly comments on current developments.

- **Valueline.com**

Founded in 1931, Value Line is the "Grand Daddy" of investment research firms, one that I referred to frequently in my banker days. The company has an excellent website, but I like to get their reports "the old fashioned way": In print! Every week I receive one of thirteen rotating Value Line Investment Surveys in the mail, each survey covering about 150 companies and updating the predecessor survey from 13 weeks before. In this fashion I have an updated review of each security I own every quarter.

Value Line follows over 1700 companies and the quality of analysis is very good, although slightly more abridged than Morningstar due primarily to space limitations. The reports make specific projections about dividend growth, which Morningstar does not do. Value Line also offers a "Safety" rating, which considers stock price stability and financial strength.

- **Valuentum.com**

Valuentum does not appear to have the breadth and depth of analytical talent that Morningstar has, and this site follows a more formula-driven approach to determine value. Nevertheless, each company receives a very detailed, rigorously formatted sixteen page analysis. Each report contains the same information in the same location, which makes it easy to collect data and compare companies.

Valuentum is clearly debt averse, which appeals to the banker in me. However, this leads them to give relatively low marks to capital intensive industries such as REITs, utilities or energy companies. However, I do like their consistency in applying their "anti-debt" standards, even if this means they are somewhat out of step with certain industries.

Valuentum also offers a separate analysis of each company's dividends, which I find extremely helpful. This is the only site I have found that calculates a "dividend cushion," which measures the safety/protection of the dividend payment.

- ## SeekingAlpha.com

Seeking Alpha is an investor blog that solicits articles from its readers. These articles cover broad topics such as investment strategy and economic/financial trends, and also offer individual stock reviews and recommendations. Some of the articles are worthless but a surprising number are quite sophisticated and instructive. Perhaps the best feature is that readers comment on each article, and often these comments are more insightful than the articles themselves. This site is particularly helpful in reviewing Real Estate Investment Trusts and Business Development Companies.

- ## Other Sources

You will find that there are dozens of sites dedicated to dividend investing. Some sites are just noise and of virtually no value. These sites will promise incredible returns – if you will just subscribe today! You will easily find a number of such sites and hopefully avoid them.

However there are other sites I have used that have been helpful. In no particular order, I would list:

- Longrundata.com: Free. This free site is excellent for dividend history going back more than 10 years.
- Parsimonyresearch.com: Fee based. Provides a detailed quantitative grading system similar to mine.
- Fastgraphs.com: Fee based. Provides graphs which help determine stock fair value/purchase timing.
- Yahoofinance.com: Free site with a wide variety of general information
- Thedividendguyblog.com: Covers both US and Canadian stocks

Mechanics of Data Collection

In order to make this book as "hands on" and practical as possible, I want to go through the specific steps required to collect the data you will need to quantify the ten metrics. Most of this data is available on Morningstar, as indicated below:

Morningstar.com

Once you have entered Morningstar.com, you will arrive at the home page. At the very top of the page is an oval surrounding "quote." Enter the symbol of the stock you want in that oval and hit return. If you do not know the symbol, enter the stock name in the oval and you will be given the symbol to enter.

Quote tab

You will be directed to the "Quote" tab for the stock you entered. As you scroll down this page you will find: "Last Price" (Left hand side) and "Latest Indicated Dividend Amount" (Right hand side). Annualize this dividend amount (multiply quarterly dividend by 4) and divide by Last Price to determine *Current Yield*. You will also find "Morningstar Premium Analyst Report" (Left hand side). If you become a premium subscriber, you will find the Economic Moat listed here, as well as the Credit and management Stewardship Rating. Also, make a note of the "Fair Value Estimate," which we will discuss when we address the issue of "When" (to buy) later.

You will also see a chart presenting "Stock Price" (left side). Hit the "10Y" button to get a ten year stock history. You will need this to calculate the *Recession Recovery Index*. Put your cursor on the highest pre-recession price and a dot will appear, along with the price and the date, which appear immediately above. Make a note of these. Then put your cursor on the lowest recession price and note this amount.

Finally put your cursor on the first post-recession price that equals the pre-recession high price, and note the date. You now have the data you need to calculate the maximum percentage price decline and the months to price recovery (one half the product is the Recession Recovery Index). *If the stock price does not recover, the RRI is zero.*

You will also notice a number of stars next to the company name. This is NOT an indication of the quality of the stock. Rather it is Morningstar's estimate as to the price of the stock relative to its intrinsic fair value. Stocks with one or two stars are overpriced. Three stars indicate a stock that is fairly priced. Three or four stars indicate that the stock is cheap and represents a good buying opportunity.

Performance tab

Next, enter the "Performance" tab (to the right of "Quote"). Here you will enter the sub-heading "Total Returns." Just below the price, hit the "Expanded View" box. You will now see ten years of total returns, needed for the *Standard Deviation calculation.* Just below that you will see a series of bar charts. The *3-year, 5-Year, and 10-Year returns* that you will need are listed here.

Return to the top of this page and hit "Dividends and Splits" (which appears directly under "Performance"). This will bring up a complete dividend history. Scroll down and open up the data for this year and the previous year. This will give you the *year-over-year dividend change*, and you can then calculate the percentage change.

Key Ratios tab

Next, enter the "Key Ratios" tab (to the right of "performance"). Here you will find *the five year dividend history* and the *five year Operating Cash Flow history*. You will need these numbers to calculate the weighted average growth rates of these two metrics. You will also find the *Dividend Payout Ratios*, which you will need to calculate the weighted 3-year average for this metric.

Finally, you can see if the number of shares outstanding has declined over the past three years.

If so, note the number of shares outstanding for this year and three years ago. You will need these to calculate the *Share Buyback yield*. If the number of shares has not declined, the Buyback Yield is zero.

Bonds tab

Finally, hit the "Bonds" tab. There you will get the *Credit Rating* (left side). Scroll down and you will get the ratio *Debt/ EBIDA*. You will also get the ratio "Debt/Equity." This is NOT the same as *Debt/Total Capital* (which is what you want), but you can use this ratio to calculate Debt/Total Capital. Just add the number 1.00 (representing relative equity) to this number (relative debt), and that will give you Total Capital (Debt + Equity). Then divide the numerator (relative debt) by this new number (debt + equity) to get the ratio you want.

Longrundata.com

Morningstar only traces dividends back ten years. This site has more extensive data to help you to trace the number of *years of consecutive dividend increases*. Enter the stock symbol and hit "Calculate Return" (you will probably have to change either Start Date or End Date – pick any recent date for either, it won't matter). In the middle of the screen you will see dividend history back to 1985 and you can trace dividend performance from this chart.

As I mentioned earlier, I consider the consecutive record intact if the company held dividends steady between two years (two years only) during the recent recession.

Be aware that the numbers are presented in dollars. If you are looking at a foreign stock, this may create a problem because exchange rates may affect the results. Frankly I would not handicap a foreign stock because of exchange rates (over which the company has no control) but it can be quite cumbersome to translate the dollar dividends back into the home country currency.

Summary

You now have the website locations you need to gather the data to measure our metrics.

I have developed a stock evaluation form that I use to collect this data, which is shown on the next page. I have indicated on the form where the data can be found. This is the primary form that I use to complete the two stock selection screens that we will discuss next.

Preliminary Common Stock Selection Screen

A stock screen establishes a series of tests or requirements that a common stock must meet in order to be considered for purchase. We will set up two screens. The *preliminary screen* establishes several broad requirements that will eliminate the great majority of common stocks from further consideration. For those companies that pass the preliminary screen, a *final screen* – far more detailed and demanding than the first – will be applied to select and rank stocks for final consideration.

The components of the preliminary screen are as follows:

Dividend History: Company must have paid a dividend continuously for the past ten years.

There can be no dividend cuts during the past seven year period.

The implicit requirement here is that the company must be at least ten years old. This first screen eliminates a large proportion of publicly traded companies, including well known companies such as Amazon (no dividends), General Electric (substantial dividend cuts in 2009 and 2010), Apple (dividends only

STOCK EVALUATION: DATE:

Symbol:

Sector:

Business:

Current Price: $ Morningstar quote

Dividend: $ Morningstar quote Payable: M Q SA A Quote

    Annual Dividend: $ Quote

Current Yield: **Calculate from annual dividend/price**

Dividend History: 2014   2013   2012   2011   2010   2009

       Morningstar key ratios

Dividend: 5 year weighted average growth rate:

       Calculate from dividend history above

Last Dividend Increase (date): **Morningstar Performance – dividends & splits**

% Last Dividend Increase (y/y): **Morningstar Performance – dividends & splits**

Estimated Dividend Growth: Next 5 years:

Morningstar **Fee Service – Only offers a limited number of quotes**

    Value Line **Fee Service**

    Valuentum **Fee Service – Requires a calculation**

    Dividend: Projected 5 Year Growth Rate: Your Decision Based On Above

5 Year Projected Yield: **Current yield compounded by your projected 5 yr growth rate**

Ave Number Shares: Last Fye: **Morningstar Key Ratios**

Ave Number Shares: Fye – 3: **Morningstar Key Ratios**

3 Year Negative Growth Rate (Buyback Yield): **Calculate from above number shares**

Dividend Payout Ratio: **Morningstar Key Ratios**   2014   2013   2012

Weighted Average Dividend Payout Ratio: **Calculate from above**

Years Consecutive Dividend Increases: **Longrundata**

Cash From Operations: 2014   2013   2012   2011   2010   2009

       Morningstar Key Ratios

5 Year Weighted Average Growth Cfo: **Calculate from above**

Moat: **Morningstar Quote (Premium Service)**

Balance Sheet: **Morningstar Bonds**

Credit Rating: **Bonds**   Debt/EBITDA: **Bonds** Debt/Total Capital: **Bonds**

Total Return: **Morningstar Performance – Total Returns**

3 Years: 5 Years: 10 Years:

3/5/10 Year Average Weighted Total Return:

Annual Total Returns: 2014 2013 2012 2011 2010 2009 2008 2007 2006 2005

       Morningstar Performance – Total Returns

10 Year Standard Deviation / Total Return:

       Calculate from above (i.e., Excel spreadsheet)

Maximum Recession Stock Price Decline: **Morningstar Quote**

Months To Recover To Pre-Recession High Stock Price: **Morningstar Quote**

Recession Recovery Index: **Calculate from above**

since 2012), and auto makers Ford and General Motors (lengthy dividend suspensions). However we do not require a 15, 20, or 25 year dividend growth history as some DGI investors prefer.

Dividend Yield: Minimum current Dividend Yield of 2.75%.

This is a good point to discuss the tradeoff between *current yield* and *dividend growth*. As we have seen, these two metrics constitute the very core of DGI. However, *depending on one's age*, an investor might prefer to emphasize one of these metrics over the other.

In general, I prefer to emphasize current yield over future dividend growth. There are two reasons for this. In the first place, I am retired and need income now. I simply don't have the time to wait for future growth to produce a satisfactory yield. The second reason is true for all investors, regardless of age:

The future is uncertain. A stock that demonstrates excellent dividend growth today may confront any number of issues that could cause future dividend growth to decline.

An example might help here:

Company A: Current dividend yield of 2.0% with strong growth projected at 12% per year.

Company B: Current dividend yield of 4.0% with weaker growth projected at 2% per year.

DIVIDENDS PAID PER $1000 INITIAL INVESTMENT										
YEARS:	1	2	3	4	5	6	7	8	9	10
Company A	20.00	22.40	25.09	28.10	31.47	35.25	39.48	44.21	49.52	55.46
Company B	40.00	40.80	41.62	42.45	43.30	44.16	45.04	45.95	46.87	47.80

Conclusion: It is not until the ninth year that the Company A dividend overtakes Company B.

Conclusion: After 10 years, Company A has paid out $350.98. Company B has paid $437.99

Conclusion: It is not until Year 14 (not shown) that total dividends from Company A exceed Company B

Notice that this projection assumes a continued compound dividend growth rate of 12% for 14 full years before total cash flow parity is achieved. That is a pretty demanding goal for any company to achieve.

Older investors need to focus on income today. However, a younger investor with a horizon of perhaps 20 years or longer to retirement should definitely focus more on growth. I think it fair to conclude that a stock with rapidly growing dividends should also produce a greater level of capital appreciation as well.

Therefore a younger investor might wish to reduce this minimum yield requirement to a level of 2.0%.

I think that anything below 2% is just too small for compounding to work effectively.

Dividend Growth: Minimum 5-year dividend Weighted Average Growth Rate of 2.0%

Every company that we consider, no matter how high its current yield, should also demonstrate a commitment to grow the dividend as well. This is the second core characteristic of DGI. We select a minimum historic 5-year growth rate that should at least equal the anticipated rate of inflation.

3-Year Weighted Average Dividend Payout Ratio: Maximum of 75%

The three-year weighted average ratio of Dividends/Earnings (Net Income) shall not exceed 75%.[27]

A higher ratio indicates that a relatively small drop in earnings might produce a reduced cash flow insufficient to cover dividends. The lower the ratio, the more comfortable the margin of dividend safety.

---

27   Dividend coverage for REITs and Master Limited Partnerships is calculated in a different manner, to be discussed. See **Attachments F and G**.

Cash Flow from Operations: 5-Year Weighted Average Growth Rate must be positive.

Cash flow is the ultimate source of dividend payments and dividend growth. We would like to see strong growth here but there are certain industries, such as utilities, where CFO tends to be relatively stable. That is consistent with a slow-growth industry with higher dividend yields but slower dividend growth. So for this preliminary screen we require only a positive number here.

Economic Moat: The company must have either a Narrow or a Wide Economic Moat.

The company should enjoy a strong competitive position and be a dominant force in its industry. It should be protected by barriers to entry and be able to produce returns on invested capital (ROIC) in excess of its cost of capital. Moat ratings are available on Morningstar / Premium membership.

Balance Sheet Strength:Investment Grade Rating (BBB- and above)

As discussed above, the Investment Grade Rating from Standard & Poor's must be at least BBB- or higher. These ratings are available for free at standardandpoors.com. Enter the company name and a rating is provided. Morningstar also provides a credit rating for larger companies.

Total Return:Weighted (3, 2, 1) Average Total Return for 10 years, 5 years, and 3 years: Minimum 6.5%

Morningstar's basic (free) service provides data for 3, 5, and 10 year total returns under the "performance" tab for any given stock. The weighted average should exceed 6.5%·

Additional metrics not considered in the preliminary screen:

- 5-Year Projected Dividend Yield
- Share Buybacks

- Years of Consecutive Dividend Increases
- Total Return Standard Deviation
- Recession Recovery
- Debt/EBITDA; Debt/Total Capitalization

These metrics will all be considered in the final screen, but I do not set up any minimum requirements for them in the primary screen as I do with the other factors listed above.

Cheating:

I can absolutely guarantee that you will be frustrated by the preliminary screen almost as soon as you begin to use it. You will find a *great* company that unfortunately fails to meet one of the requirements of the screen. I debated over this and finally decided to permit cheating. But only limited cheating!

If a company fails to meet *one and only one* of the preliminary screen requirements, it may still be considered for the final screen. If the company fails to meet two requirements, it will be eliminated.

Finding companies to screen:

We have established our preliminary screen, and now we are ready to select companies to screen.

Let me save you a great deal of effort. There are literally hundreds of sources that you could use to develop a list of dividend paying companies to screen. However I would suggest that you begin by considering the following companies:

- Dividend Champions – 106 US companies that have raised dividends for 25+ consecutive years
- Dividend Contenders – 250 US companies that have raised dividends for 10 – 24 years
- Dividend Challengers – 281 US companies that have raised dividends for 5 – 9 years

These lists are available at *dripinvesting.org/tools*. Under "Information," hit "PDF Format."

These spread sheets contain an incredible amount of dividend data – virtually all that you will need to complete the primary screen. It is a fabulous resource, and it's free! So there are 637 companies right off the top to keep you busy!

Foreign companies:

You will notice that the above lists include very few foreign companies, so this would be an appropriate place for me to comment on investments in foreign corporations.

I am out of step with the great majority of investment advisors who advocate some not insignificant exposure to foreign stocks to achieve geographic diversification. In addition to the obvious foreign exchange risk of being paid non-dollar dividends, I have several concerns about this advice:

- Foreign companies do not have the same level of commitment to stable or increasing dividend payments that US companies have. Foreign dividends tend to rise and fall with current earnings.
- Foreign dividends may be paid only once or twice a year. This means delayed payments and lost reinvestment opportunities, but it also becomes harder to project the trend of future payments.
- Foreign dividends may be subjected to significant withholding taxes. You may receive a credit for some/all of these taxes on your US tax return, but this is still a complication.
- Foreign accounting standards are not as rigorous as US standards and financial statements can be more difficult to interpret or understand.
- Foreign financial markets are not as mature, liquid, or regulated as US markets.
- Foreign governments can be despotic, unstable, and unfriendly. Russia anyone?

Preliminary Stock Screen – Summary:

Here then are the metrics for our preliminary stock selection screen. Listed again are the Morningstar tabs where the required data may be found.

Metric	Morningstar Tab
Minimum ten year dividend history	Key Ratios
No dividend cuts during the past seven years	Key Ratios
Minimum current dividend yield of 2.75%	Quote
Minimum 5-year wt. ave. dividend growth rate of 2.0%	Key Ratios (Calculation needed)
Max. 3-year weighted average dividend pay-out ratio: 75%	Key Ratios (Calculation needed)
Five year growth rate: Cash From Operations: Positive	Key Ratios (Calculation needed)
Economic Moat: Narrow or Wide	Quote (Premium)
Investment grade credit rating	Bonds
Minimum Weighted Average 3-5-10 year Total Return: 6.5%	Performance

Preliminary Stock Screen – Case Studies

I have selected six companies that we will follow through the Preliminary Screen process as well as the Final Screen protocol. In selecting these companies I tried to differentiate them by industry, size, age, dividend history and growth, financial and competitive strength, and total return. I hope that these companies will give you a good feel for the entire stock selection process and some of the unique considerations and decisions that you will face as you proceed through the protocol.

Microsoft (MSFT)

Microsoft is a leading developer of computer software for both consumer and commercial uses.

Sector: Technology

Founded: 1975
Revenue: $87B

General Mills (GIS)

General Mills is a leading global manufacturer of branded food products.

Sector: Consumer Staples
Founded: 1928
Revenue: $17B

Chevron (CVX)

Chevron is the second largest fully integrated US oil/gas company.

Sector: Energy
Founded: 1879
Revenue: $266B

Emerson Electric (EMR)

Emerson Electric manufactures electric motors, controls, and monitors.

Sector: Industrials
Founded: 1890
Revenue: $24B

Johnson & Johnson (JNJ)

Johnson & Johnson is engaged in the research and manufacture of a wide variety of healthcare products.

Sector: Healthcare
Founded: 1886
Revenue: $74B

Westar Energy (WR)

Westar Energy is the largest electric utility in Kansas.

Sector: Electric Utility
Founded: 1924
Revenue: $2.6B

PRELIMINARY SCREEN RESULTS
SEPTEMBER 2015

	MSFT	GIS	CVX	EMR	JNJ	WR
Minimum Dividend History (10 Yrs)	Yes	Yes	Yes	Yes	Yes	Yes
No Dividend Cuts (7 Years)	Yes	Yes	Yes	Yes	Yes	Yes
Dividend Yield (Minimum 2.75%)	2.88%	3.00%	5.39%	4.06%	3.07%	3.95%
5-Yr Wt Av Div Growth Rate (Min 2.0%)	17.6%	11.2%	9.9%	6.0%	7.1%	3.1%
3-Yr Wt Ave Div Payout Ratio (Max 75%)	.447	.613	.338	.581	.518	.589
5 Yr Wt Ave Growth Rate: CFO (Positive)	1.2%	6.5%	1.3%	4.7%	5.4%	8.3%
Economic Moat (Narrow or Wide)	W	N	N	N	W	N
Credit Rating (Above BBB-)	AAA	A	AA-	A+	AAA	BBB+
Wt Average Total Return (Min 6.5%)	11.8%	12.6%	**4.4%***	8.7%	9.4%	9.1%

* Below minimum requirement

Review of the Preliminary Screen results:

Microsoft (MSFT)

Microsoft has the lowest dividend yield, which is not surprising given that it is still a young company and tech companies are not big dividend payers. The dividend growth rate is exceptional; the payout ratio and total return numbers are very strong. Wide moat with AAA credit. Advance to the final screen.

General Mills (GIS)

General Mills has the second lowest dividend, offset by the second best dividend growth rate. The payout ratio is high but still well within our limit. Advance to final screen.

Chevron (CVX)

Chevron's yield is now as high as it has been in years. Unfortunately for existing shareholders (like me), this is due to a 38% stock price decline over the past year due to the unexpected and very dramatic drop in the price of oil. However, a new buyer may find this yield very enticing. Chevron is a very strong company, and except for an anemic total return (cause by the stock price drop), Chevron passes all the preliminary screen tests. We will "cheat" on this one and pass Chevron into the final screen. I think you may be glad that we did.

Emerson Electric (EMR)

This dividend stalwart has raised its dividend consecutively every year for over half a century. Solid yield. Passes all tests well within the limits. Advance to final screen.

Johnson and Johnson (JNJ)

My favorite company in the healthcare industry. Like Emerson Electric, JNJ has increased its dividends every year for over half a century. This "no brainer" advances to the final screen.

Westar Electric (WR)

I thought I should include at least one "sleeper" that most people wouldn't know. This is one of my favorite utilities with a very solid track record. Very strong total return and excellent CFO growth rate, which is unusual for a utility. Advance to final screen.

Final Stock Selection Screen

We now return to the two basic challenges of picking stocks:

- We have established a list of ten metrics with which to evaluate securities. How do we determine the relative importance – or weight – which we will assign to each metric?
- Once we have assigned weights, how do we evaluate these metrics within a single, comprehensive, quantitative format that will determine which stocks are best to buy?

Assigning Weights:

We are going to establish a quantitative model to evaluate stocks based on a total score of 1000.

Each of our ten metrics will be given a weight, which will represent that portion of the total score allocated to that metric. We assign these weights to reflect the importance we attribute to each metric.

These weights are assigned in a completely subjective manner. There is no "right" or "wrong" allocation of weights: The allocation depends solely on the judgment of the weight assignor! You may feel that certain metrics should have a stronger or weaker weight than I do. The weights presented below are my weights, and you are completely free to reassign them as you see fit.

I break the ten metrics into three basic categories and assign the following weights to these categories:

- Dividend Yield and Growth: 400 points
- Dividend Protection: 440 points
- Stock Performance: <u>160 points</u>
                  TOTAL: 1000 points

I break these weights down as follows into the individual metrics:

Dividend Yield and Growth

Dividend Yield:	200 points
5 year Projected Yield:	150 points
Share Buybacks:	50 points
TOTAL:	400 points

Dividend Protection

Dividend Payout Ratio:	150 points
Balance Sheet:	150 points
5 Yr Wt. Ave. Growth CFO:	70 points
Yrs Consecutive Div Increases:	70 points
TOTAL:	440 points

Stock performance

3-5-10 Yr Weighted Ave.

Total Return:	80 points
10 Year Standard Deviation:	40 points
Recession Recovery Index:	40 points
TOTAL:	160 points

The weights I have assigned begin with a total weighting of 350 points for current and projected yield.

This is approximately one third of the total amount. I initially placed a higher weight on these two metrics but ultimately decided not to get too "greedy" here (which is very easy to do!). I placed a much lower weight on share buybacks, which, while certainly of benefit to shareholders, are not in my opinion nearly as significant as direct cash payments.

I wanted dividend protection to have the highest weight, which it does with 440 points. This weighting comes from my concern that dividend investors may put too much emphasis on yield, and not enough on *protection* of that yield. "Chasing yield" is a very easy trap to fall into and there are any number of stocks you could find with yields in excess of 10% and higher. I would urge great caution here. That is why I want more weight on protection than on yield itself.

All investors like to see their stocks perform well in terms of total return. While price appreciation is not our primary goal, I still wanted some weighting for overall performance. This sector therefore has a total weight of 160 points, or 16% of the total.

Constructing the Model: Multipliers

So we have now reached a point where we have:

- Selected the metrics we want to use to evaluate stocks
- Collected data from Morningstar and other sources for these metrics
- Established weights for these metrics based on a total (perfect) score of 1000

So the final question is: How do we tie all this together? How do we convert raw data into specific point scores within the model?

This brings us to a discussion of "multipliers." "Multipliers" is the term I give to numbers which convert raw data into a specific score within the model. I think the best way to present this is with an example.

Let's begin with the first metric, Dividend Yield. We have a specific value for this metric: Let's say 3.50%. We want to translate that data value into a specific point score. *Keep in mind that the maximum possible score for Dividend Yield is 200 points, which is the weight we have assigned.*

What we have to do first is to *pick a dividend yield that will convert to the maximum score.* This will in effect be our "cut off" yield in that we would be perfectly happy with this yield, but we would recognize that any yield above this would be superfluous – *it would not produce a higher point score.*

Just to start this process, let's say that we pick a 10% yield to convert to a maximum score. We would then divide 200 points by 10 to produce the Multiplier 20. So 10 times the Multiplier (20) equals the maximum score of 200. Any yield higher than 10% would also score 200 points, the maximum for this metric. *So yields above 10% -- the cut off yield – would not produce a higher score for this stock.*

But here is the issue: If our multiplier is 20, then a dividend of 3.50% translates into a score of 70. This is a very low point score out of a maximum of 200. So stocks with decent yields around 3-4% are going to have very low scores compared to very high yield (riskier) stocks. Unless these lower yielding stocks are *much* stronger in terms of the other metrics, a multiplier set this low would make it very difficult for lower yielding stocks to have a total score competitive with high yielding stocks.

So that leads me to select a *lower* "cut off" yield that produces a *higher* Multiplier – in effect giving lower yielding stocks a better chance. After much experimentation with this issue, I have finally settled on a Multiplier of 37, which means that my cut off yield is 200/37 = 5.40%. I am totally happy with this yield, which I think is an excellent return for my portfolio. I recognize that higher yields will add nothing more to the score, but that is OK with me. It also means that a stock with a very decent yield of 3.50% will score 3.50 X 37 = 130, which may not be a high score but is still a reasonable score to begin with.

So the process of selecting a Multiplier is *basically a process of trial-and-error.* If you begin by selecting Multipliers that are too low – as I did – you will reward only the highest performing stocks. But you will soon discover that there simply aren't enough quality stocks in existence to satisfy these very high standards. If you select Multipliers that are too high, you will reward too many mediocre or poor stocks. So eventually you will come to some compromise in the middle where you are satisfied with a relatively high level of return without unduly handicapping adequate performance.

Constructing the Model: Dividers

You will notice that for certain metrics such as the Dividend Payout Ratio or the Standard Deviation, a lower score is preferable. In these cases a Multiplier will not work, and in fact the exact opposite is needed. In these cases we use a Divider. Again, an example will make this clear.

Looking at the Dividend Payout Ratio, I would consider any score under .40 to be a very good score. Let us take .36 as our cut off value, with 150 as our maximum score. So to convert .36 to a maximum score, and *recognizing that higher payout ratios must produce lower scores*, we calculate a Divider of .36 X 150 = 54. The Divider becomes the numerator and our data (expressed as a decimal) becomes the denominator as follows: 54/.36 = 150.

The Standard Deviation test is another metric that requires a Divider. Here I look to a low STDEV of 12.0% as being my cut off score, with 40 as my maximum score. So my Divider is 12.0 X 40 = 480.

Here then is a table that summarizes the Multipliers and Dividers that I now use. Again, these are subjective numbers and – just like the weightings we discussed earlier – you may want to adjust these figures to reflect your own preferences.

Metric	Multiplier/ Divider	Maximum Score	Cut Off Data Value
Current Yield:	37X	200	5.40%
5 Year Projected Yield:	24X	150	6.25%
Share Buyback Yield:	22X	50	2.27%
Dividend Payout:	54/	150	0.36
5 Year Growth CFO:	8X	70	8.75%
Yrs Consecutive Div Increase:	5X	70	14
3-5-10 Yr Wt Ave Total Return:	7X	80	11.4%
10 Year Standard Deviation:	480/	40	12.0%
Recession Recovery Index:	24,000/	40	600

There is one metric left, the balance sheet, which has a different scoring system.

Balance Sheet

This is the most complicated metric to convert into a single point score because there are actually three separate "sub metrics" within this category to consider. So in this case we will use a table which will establish a point value for each of the three sub metrics: (Maximum Score: 150)

BALANCE SHEET EVALUATION TABLE
METRICS

CREDIT RATING		DEBT/EBITDA		DEBT/TOTAL CAPITAL	
RATING	SCORE	VALUE	SCORE	VALUE	SCORE
AAA	75	0.00–1.00	50	.00–.15	25
AA+	73	1.01–1.50	47	.16–.20	24
AA	70	1.51–2.00	44	.21–.25	23
AA-	67	2.01–2.50	41	.26–.30	22
A+	65	2.51–2.75	38	.31–.35	20
A	63	2.76–3.00	35	.36–.40	18
A-	60	3.01–3.25	32	.41–.45	16
BBB+	55	3.26–3.50	29	.46–.50	14
BBB	50	3.51–3.75	27	.51–.55	12
BBB-	45	3.76–4.00	25	.56–.60	10
		4.01–4.50	23	.61–.65	8
Below Investment Grade:		4.51–5.00	20	.66–.70	6
BB+	30	5.01–5.50	17	.71–.75	4
BB	20	5.51–6.00	14	Over .75	0
BB-	10	6.01–6.50	10		
Below BB-:	0	6.51–7.00	6		
		Over 7.00	0		

Two quick examples:

Microsoft has a very strong balance sheet:

Credit Rating:	AAA	Score: 75
Debt/EBITDA:	1.40	Score: 47
Debt/Total Capital:	0.30	Score: <u>22</u>
TOTAL SCORE:		144/150

As a utility, Westar Energy has more debt:

Credit Rating:	BBB+	Score: 55
Debt/EBITDA:	3.68	Score: 27
Debt/Total Capital:	0.50	Score: <u>14</u>
TOTAL SCORE:		96/150

Completion of our model

We have completed the construction of our model in four basic steps:

- Selected the metrics to evaluate stocks
- Assembled the data/values for these metrics
- Assigned weights to the metrics
- Developed a model to convert data values into point scores

We have used the Stock Evaluation form previously shown (page 134) to collect the data for our six case studies. This data is presented in the table below. The ten scoring matrices are bolded and highlighted in gray:

FINAL SCREEN DATA

	MSFT	GIS	CVX	EMR	JNJ	WR
Dividend Yield	2.88%	3.00%	5.39%	4.06%	3.07%	3.95%
5 Yr Wt Ave Dividend Growth	17.6%	11.2%	9.90%	6.05%	7.14%	3.07%
Last Y/Y Dividend Increase	10.7%	7.3%	7.0%	9.3%	7.1%	2.9%
Est Div Growth: Next 5 Yrs	12.0%	6.5%	5.0%	7.0%	6.5%	3.5%
Projected 5 Yr Dividend Yield	5.08%	4.11%	6.88%	5.69%	4.21%	4.69%
Ave # Shares: Fye 2014	8254	619	1898	695	2864	130
Ave # Shares: Fye 2011	8506	667	2001	754	2775	117
Buyback Yield	1.00%	2.46%	1.75%	2.30	NONE	NONE
Div Payout Ratio FYE 2014	.490	.716	.381	.476	.451	.588
Div Payout Ratio FYE 2013	.383	.538	.311	.794	.566	.578
Div Payout Ratio FYE 2012	.445	.475	.264	.471	.622	.612
3 Yr Weighted Ave Div Payout Ratio	**.447**	**.613**	**.338**	**.581**	**.518**	**.589**
Years Consecutive Div Increase	11	10	27	57	52	12
5 Yr Wt Ave Growth: CFO	1.24%	6.52%	1.32%	4.69%	5.40%	8.30%
Credit Rating	AAA	A	AA-	A+	AAA	BBB+
Debt/EBITDA	1.40	3.44	0.82	1.25	0.81	3.68
Debt/Total Capital	.30	.65	.17	.43	.21	.50
Balance Sheet Score:	144	100	141	128	148	96
Total Return: 3 Yrs	17.6%	17.0%	-4.7%	11.9%	14.5%	10.8%
Total Return: 5 Yrs	15.9%	7.6%	12.2%	6.1%	11.9%	11.6%
Total Return: 10 Yrs	7.2%	8.3%	11.5%	6.4%	5.9%	6.9%
3/5/10/Yr Wt Ave Total Return	11.8%	12.6%	4.4%	8.7%	9.3%	9.1%
10 Yr Standard Deviation: TR	28.84	9.00	18.89	23.61	12.50	15.54
Max Recession Stock Price Drop	56.1%	27.4%	38.7%	54.0%	29.0%	8.6%
Mos To Recover Pre-Recess Hi	73	13	33	56	52	50
Recession Recovery Index	2047	178	638	1512	754	965

Scoring

We have now completed all data collection and calculation. We are – at last! – ready to determine the model score for each of our six companies, and then compare these scores to determine the most attractive candidates for portfolio selection.

Below is the *scoring matrix* that I use to determine the final score for each stock. I copy this matrix directly on the back of the *stock evaluation form* (page 134) for each company so that I have all my data and scoring calculations on the same sheet of paper. I have filled the form in with the data from Microsoft to demonstrate how this is used.

Note that the "Mult/Divid" column (Multiplier/Divider) and the "Max Score" (maximum score allocated to this metric) remain the same for all stocks.

SCORING MATRIX
COMPANY:MICROSOFT

Metric	Data Value	Mult/ Divid	Score	Max Score	Final Score
Dividend Yield and Growth					
Current Yield (%):	2.88	37X	107	200	107
Projected 5 year yield (%):	5.08	24X	122	150	122
Share Buyback yield (%):	1.00	22X	22	50	22
Dividend Protection					
Dividend Payout Ratio:	.447	54/	121	150	121
Balance Sheet:		see table	144	150	144
5 Yr Wt Ave Growth CFO (%):	1.24	8X	10	70	10
Years Dividend Increase:	11	5X	55	70	55
Stock Performance					
Wt Ave 3-5-10 Total Return	11.8	7X	83	80	80
10 Yr Standard Deviation	28.84	480/	17	40	17
Recession Recovery Index	2047	24,000/	12	40	12
TOTAL SCORE				1000	**690**

Please note that the Microsoft score for 3-5-10 year Total Return (83) exceeded the maximum for this metric (80) so the final score was limited to the maximum score.

The table below displays the final model scores for all six of our companies.

FINAL SCORES

Metric	Maximum Score	MSFT	GIS	CVX	EMR	JNJ	WR
Yield (X37)	200	107	111	199	150	114	146
5 Yr Yield (X23)	150	122	95	150^M	131	97	108
Buyback Yield (X22)	50	22	50^M	38	50^M	0	0
Div Payout Ratio (54/)	150	121	88	150^M	93	104	92
Balance Sheet	150	144	100	141	128	148	96
5 Yr Growth Cfo (X8)	70	10	52	10	38	43	66
Consec Div Incrs (X5)	70	55	50	70^M	70^M	70^M	60
3/5/10/ Wt Ave Tr (X7)	80	80^M	80^M	31	61	65	64
10 Yr Tr St Dev (480/)	40	17	40^M	25	20	38	31
Recess Recov (24,000/)	40	12	40^M	38	16	32	25
Total Score	**1000**	**690**	**706**	**852**	**757**	**711**	**688**

M = Maximum Score exceeded

Results of the Final Screen:

Our case study stocks are all high quality, established firms that passed successfully through a Preliminary Stock Selection Screen. It would be fair to assume that they would score reasonably well in the final screen, and that is in fact the case. However, there are some clear differences between the companies that enable us to establish a ranking/preference order.

Having worked with this system for the past few years, I have developed a ranking for final scores, which is as follows:

FINAL SCORE RANKINGS

OVER 750:	VERY STRONG
700-749:	STRONG
650-699:	NEUTRAL
600-649:	WEAK
BELOW 600:	VERY WEAK

Please note that I do not use this final screen alone to establish a "buy," "sell," or "hold" recommendation. *That is because this numeric score represents only half of the ultimate buy/sell decision: the quantitative half. We have to consider the qualitative side as well* before any such decision can be made in a comprehensive manner.

So here is the final review of our six case study stocks, including both the quantitative scores listed above along with the qualitative findings that I think relate and pertain to each stock.

Final Review: Quantitative and Qualitative Considerations

Here are the final quantitative and qualitative investment considerations relating to our six case studies. I am going to start with the lowest scoring stocks first and then move up to the higher rankings.

Westar Electric: Score 688
Quantitative Rank: Neutral +
Qualitative Considerations:

Utility stocks have higher debt levels, lower dividend growth, and no buyback yield. It would be rare for utility stocks to score much into the 700 level. Nevertheless they are excellent defensive stocks. Westar is completing a period of substantial expansion and retrofitting, and high levels of capital spending should be tapering off. Cash flow growth – already quite high for a utility – and dividend growth should accelerate. I would consider this stock for purchase.

Microsoft: Score 690
Quantitative Rank: Neutral +
Qualitative Considerations:

Microsoft is the world's largest independent manufacturer of software with revenues split about 45/55 between consumer and commercial customers. The company is an incredible cash cow, although revenue and CFO growth have slowed considerably in recent years. Dividend growth and coverage are extremely strong.

My main concern with Microsoft has been its highly unsuccessful attempt to enter the cell phone market through its acquisition of Nokia. Instead of developing software, Microsoft has shifted its focus somewhat to begin selling physical "things"

– things that have an extraordinary short product life. The result was an emormous multi-billion dollar write-down taken in 2015.

I would consider Microsoft to be a very solid "hold" for investors who already own this stock. I would be less enthusiastic about buying the stock pending the results of the release of Windows 10 and the ongoing conversion to cloud-based products.

General Mills: Score 706
Quantitative Rank: Strong -
Qualitative Considerations:

This global manufacturer of breakfast cereals and baking products has always faced competition from generic products, but strong brand loyalty has generally kept such competitors at bay. However, sales of leading cereal lines (Cheerios, Wheaties) and snack foods have been sluggish due to health concerns with high-carbohydrate, high-sugar foods.

Given that consumer tastes appear to be changing, I would consider this company to be a "hold" for existing shareholders but I am not particularly enthusiastic about buying it.

Johnson & Johnson: Score 711
Quantitative Rank:Strong –
Qualitative Considerations:

I cannot recall *ever* reading or hearing anything particularly negative about this company. This company is just quality from start to finish. According to Value Line, "JNJ is among the select few stocks in the 1700 member Value Line group that carry our Highest Marks for Safety (1) and Financial Strength (A++), Stock Price Stability, and Earnings Predictability." According to Morningstar, "Johnson & Johnson stands alone as a leader across the major health-care industries. The company's diverse revenue base, strong pipeline, and robust cash flow generation create a very wide economic moat." Etcetera Etcetera. I would strongly consider buying this stock as a core holding in virtually any portfolio.

Emerson Electric: Score 757
Quantitative Rank:Very Strong –
Qualitative Considerations:

Another very fine company. There are only four other US public companies that have a longer record of consecutive dividend increases. The company has consistently generated strong returns on invested capital, even during the 2008-09 recession. The company enjoys a wide economic moat, supported by higher customer switching costs, a streamlined cost structure, and brand loyalty. Nevertheless, recent financial results have been sluggish, the share price has dropped, and certain restructuring efforts are now in progress. The drop in price has created a current yield (4.06%) that is far above the 5 year average yield (2.7%), and I think that the timing might be right to open a position in this stock.

Chevron: Score 852
Quantitative Rank:Very Strong
Qualitative Considerations:

Chevron has an exceptionally high quantitative score that literally screams "buy me!" Virtually all ten metrics (except CFO growth) are at or near the maximum level. I have never seen a stock that combines a yield well in excess of 5%, an extraordinarily strong balance sheet, a 27-year record of consecutive dividend increases, and a payout ratio below .40! Indeed, this would appear to be a "no brainer" buy!

But here is where the qualitative side comes in and says: "Not so fast!"

In the fall of 2014 the price of crude oil fell by 50% virtually overnight. No one saw this coming. And the price has generally stayed below $50/barrel ever since. This has obviously put tremendous pressure on all energy companies, particularly the "upstream" firms that are involved in the drilling and extraction of oil. As a fully integrated oil company, Chevron has been hit hard and recent profits have been drastically reduced.

Chevron is taking a long run view of this situation. The company – all oil companies – have been through cyclical gyrations in oil prices before. Chevron and other oil producers believe that supply and demand will eventually come into balance, perhaps in the area of $70-75/barrel. And so Chevron has continued with a robust capital spending budget to locate and develop new oil fields. In doing so, they have in effect "spent" their CFO, and dividend coverage – *as measure by cash flow instead of earnings*[28] – is now negative. Chevron predicts that it will generate adequate cash flow to cover dividends in two years.

And so, what does an investor do? The historic numbers look great, the balance sheet is great, the dividend payment record is great, and management has publically stated that they will protect the dividend as their highest priority. That means borrowing to pay the dividend if necessary, great for shareholders in the short run, but the last thing any conservative company wants to do, since this cannot be sustained indefinitely.

So here is the basic quandary. If you consider *buying the stock now,* you are subjecting yourself to a *higher risk/reward* scenario. The oil market is now in a state of near-chaos and no one can predict when – or even if – recovery will be achieved. But in return for that risk, you will be buying the stock of a quality company at a bargain basement price with a yield far higher than normal. If you like the company but not the risk, *you will wait until the oil market settles down* and the recovery is much closer at hand. You will reduce your risk, but by then *the stock price will probably be higher and the yield lower.*

---

28   See **Attachment H**.

I want to make two basic points here. The first point is that *there is no correct answer.* This is a completely personal decision that depends on your own life circumstances, health, age, financial profile, and risk preferences. The second point is that *you now have the data and analysis that you need to reach an intelligent, informed, and balanced decision, whatever that decision may be.*

> **You have applied the protocol.**
> **You have considered all the appropriate quantitative**
> **and qualitative factors.**
> **You have "Walked the Walk."**
> **You have joined us as a Dividend Growth Investor.**

To state what is obvious, the stock evaluation model I have constructed and presented in this chapter is *my model*. It is all about me – my preferences, my age, my budget, my income, my attitude toward risk and reward. But *you are not me, and you should have a model that reflects you, not me.*

Depending on your own personality, your own circumstances, *your own life*, you may decide that you want to change some of my decisions and build your own model.

> **And now you know how to do that.**

You may wish to reconfigure my model by:

- Changing the metrics I have chosen to measure corporate strength;
- Changing the weights I have assigned to the metrics;
- Changing the values of the Multipliers and Dividers;
- Changing the values of the Final Score Rankings presented above (page 154)

And in so doing you will – probably after several variations and permutations – develop a model that works for you.

And that is what this book seeks to accomplish.

A rigorous quantitative discipline – a personalized discipline – that you will apply to every security

And in using your model, you will avoid the irrational, emotional, superficial decisions that destroy the building of a solid, consistent, balanced portfolio.

Diversification

We have now constructed a model to evaluate C Corporations, Real Estate Investments Trusts, and Master Limited Partnerships. As you begin to use this model and build up an inventory of potential securities to purchase, you will probably begin to see certain patterns emerge among the three asset classes covered in this section.

In general, you will find that REITs and MLPs tend to produce the highest scores. The average score for the REITs that I own is just over 790. MLPs also score high, with an average score in my portfolio of 770. By contrast, the average score for the C Corporations I have purchased is 725.

Why the difference? Well, as you might quickly guess, REITs and MLPs are relatively new asset classes that appeal primarily to income investors (like us) by offering high payouts, high yields, and strong dividend growth. Since these metrics receive the highest weights in our model, REITs and MLPs have a pronounced advantage over C Corporations. C Corps generally have better balance sheets, lower standard deviations, and longer track records of consecutive dividend increases. However, these stronger metrics receive lower weights, so in the final analysis REITs and MLPs produce higher scores.

Here again I mention that these are *my* metrics and *my* weights. If an investor wanted to stress a stronger financial position, lower volatility, and better dividend protection, the resulting scores would certainly shift more in favor of C Corporations.

But looking at the scores that my weights generate, one might be tempted to load up on REITs and MLPs. And if an investor relied strictly on the numeric scores alone, that would be a logical decision.

But concentration increases risk. The more eggs we put in one basket, the more loss we experience if that one basket fails to perform.

Up to this point we have considered the qualitative and quantitative risks of owning a particular stock. We could say that these are the *micro* risks involved in investing; that is, the risks that any one particular security might not perform. What we now need to consider are the *macro* risks of investing, meaning the *risk that our entire portfolio might not perform properly unless it has a certain balance.* This brings us to a discussion of *diversification.*

The overall purpose of diversification is quite simple: *We are spreading the risk.* If we have too much of any "one thing" and that "one thing" goes bad, then we are obviously hurt more than if we held a broad portfolio made up of securities with low price/performance correlation.

In order to keep a broad balance in my portfolio, I diversify based on three separate criteria:

- Total number of securities in the portfolio
- Diversification by asset class
- Diversification by industrial sector

Total Number of Securities:

The more securities you own, the more protection you have if any one security fails to perform. That is pretty obvious. However, as you continue to add more securities, you eventually reach a point of diminishing returns. If you already own 50 securities, you achieve very little additional protection by adding a 51st security. But you have to go through just as much work to add that 51st security as you did when you added your 5th security. So you are getting very little "bang for your buck" at that point.

There is no correct answer to the "how many" question. I think most investors would want to hold at least 20 securities in their portfolio, and I think the upper limit is about 50. I hold near the upper limit, but as I am retired I have more time to devote to portfolio maintenance and I enjoy the process. If you are more inclined to invest in funds, then for diversification purposes you could hold a far smaller number of funds compared to individual stocks.

Diversification by Asset Class:

My diversification by asset class is now as follows:

C Corporations (common and preferred stocks):	50%
Real Estate Investment Trusts:	15%
Master Limited Partnerships:	10%
High Yield (Bonds and BDCs):	10%
Municipal Bonds:	10%
Cash:	5%
	100%

I would point out again that I have a very light allocation in bonds. I own no US Treasury securities and no high grade corporate bonds. Through a closed end fund I do own a position in municipal bonds where leverage boosts my yield to about 6%. I also have a position in high yield bonds, again through two closed end funds. As I explained, any significant allocation to higher grade bonds would reduce my income below the 100% organic level and require me to periodically sell securities to pay my bills. An allocation to high credit bonds might be a good defensive move *if I were focused on capital preservation* as my primary objective, but that is *not* my objective, and *I am not willing to give up full income coverage – which I have – for the sake of diversification designed to protect price.*

I also have a relatively small cash position and remain pretty much fully invested. The obvious reason is of course to boost income. I do sacrifice the ability to pick up good bargains during a market downturn (unless I sell something to buy something else), but I am not going to sacrifice income in order to speculate on market timing.

Diversification by Industry Sector:

In addition to asset class diversity, I also want to diversify by industrial sector, and in particular I want a strong position in defensive stocks. At present, my sector allocation is as follows:

My Sector Diversification

Cyclical:	26%	Sensitive:	40%	Defensive:	34%
Real Estate	15%	Energy	15%	Utilities	16%
Finance	6%	Teleco	10%	Healthcare	10%
Consumer	5%	Technology	8%	Consumer	8%
		Industrials	7%		

By comparison, here is the sector diversification that now exists within all S&P 500 stocks:

S&P 500 Sector Diversification (July 2015)
Source: Morningstar.com

Cyclical:	31%	Sensitive:	41%	Defensive:	28%
Finance	15%	Technology	18%	Healthcare	16%
Consumer	11%	Industrials	11%	Consumer	9%
Materials	3%	Energy	8%	Utilities	3%
Real Estate	2%	Telecom	4%		

The differences between my allocation and the S&P become clear very quickly. In the cyclical sector, I am much heavier in real estate, given its advantages to the income investor. Yet because I avoid banks and basic materials, my overall exposure in the cyclical sector is below the S&P, which is where I want it.

In the sensitive sector, I am heavy in energy and telecoms, but light in technology, a sector with less appeal for income investors. However, my overall exposure to sensitive stocks is virtually the same as the S&P, again a position that I am comfortable with. Finally, I am quite heavy in utilities, which offer higher yields and consistent cash flow, so my defensive position is relatively high.

So the big picture for my portfolio diversification is a moderate shift away from the cyclical and toward the defensive, with the middle remaining stationary. I think this makes sense for a conservative income investor, *particularly an investor who has entered retirement*. A younger investor could potentially digest several major cyclical movements, but I can't!

Measuring Your Diversification:

Unless you have only a few stocks in your portfolio, it will be a difficult task to keep accurate track of diversification. Fortunately there is an easy solution for this. If you become a member of Morningstar, you may register your entire portfolio on that site. This will provide you with instant pricing for the portfolio throughout the trading day. There are also numerous tools that Morningstar provides to monitor your portfolio, including – with premium membership – a complete breakdown of portfolio diversification. Hit the "Portfolio" tab on the top toolbar and then hit "X-Ray." This will provide a complete breakdown of your portfolio by asset class, stock sector, stock style, and stock type. It will also show the yield, P/E ratio, and return on equity for the entire portfolio. If you own any investment funds, X-Ray will also break down all the individual holdings of that fund and sort each holding into the proper diversification category. That is *certainly* something that you could not do by hand!

Summary:

In order to achieve proper diversification, the investor needs to establish dollar or percentage limits for each asset class and industrial sector. Then, within each class/sector, he can select securities based on the qualitative and quantitative criteria we have established. This will mean that certain lower-scoring stocks may be selected over higher-scoring stocks if they belong to different classes/sectors. This would happen if the higher-scoring stock belongs in an asset class that has already reached its maximum limit.

I think that diversification ultimately depends on three primary factors:

- Age – Younger investors need less current income and can absorb more cyclical exposure
- Risk/Reward attitude and tolerance
- Level of "income independence" – How close are you to a 100% organic portfolio?

Regarding the last factor: If your portfolio – combined with other income sources – is capable of providing sufficient income to cover all your living expenses plus inflation (you are 100% organic); then you need to be less concerned with *macro* diversification (asset class/sector) as long as you are very comfortable with your *micro* diversification. Since you should not have to sell any securities (except perhaps for extraordinary expenses), then price sensitivity becomes a lower priority. On the other hand, to the extent that you are short of a 100% organic position, then macro diversification becomes more important, as securities must be sold to close the income gap.

Summary: Section Three

Sooner or later, every investor will come across a stock that they just *have* to buy. It may be a tip from an old friend who "really knows the market." It may be an exciting new product that you just *know* is going to take off. Perhaps it's a company that your sister works for, who has some "inside information" from her boss. Whatever it may be, you are totally jazzed and ready to pull the trigger!

Believe me, I have "been there, done that."
No protocol, no discipline, no analysis – just buy it!

So here's my horror story, from the good old days at the end of the last century. In 1998 I purchased a high tech growth fund at a price of $35. I did no research at all – I just wanted to jump on board the Dot Com Express! Over the next year that fund more than tripled in value to over $120. Then the bleeding started in 2000. I watched the price fall over 80% and eventually bailed out at $22. And naturally I did not receive one penny in dividends. A 37% loss. It could have been much worse.

The purpose of this section is to establish a discipline – a protocol – that you will apply to *every* stock in *every* situation, no matter how exciting the opportunity may appear. It is frankly hard to do this. It means that you can never let your emotions run away with you – you can't let yourself get carried away. Not easy. Not at all.

Some investors are able to set aside part of their portfolio as "mad money" – money that they can simply gamble with. To me, that's harder than a strictly observed protocol, because once you introduce "no rules" investing, where do you stop? Such an approach would not work for me.

I have selected ten metrics to evaluate stocks. I have assigned weights to these metrics which represent their importance to me. I have established a model to convert metric data into numeric scores to compare stocks. But it may well be that *you* would prefer to exclude some of these metrics or include others. *You* may wish to assign different weights. *You* may want to establish different multipliers or dividers.

And that is exactly what I hope you will do. Make the model work for you. Customize it as you see fit.

It may take you several attempts over several months to feel comfortable with it, just as it did for me. In fact, I am still fine tuning it even after three years. *But the more you make it your model, the more you will feel comfortable using it.* Using it with *every* stock – no gambling allowed! – I hope!

SECTION FOUR

HOW:
Investment Funds

What This Section Will Cover

In the last section we set up a system to evaluate individual securities – corporations and partnerships. We now want to turn our attention to investment funds – open-end, closed-end, and exchange-traded, and determine another approach – another protocol – to evaluate this type of security. This approach will have to focus on different metrics since investment funds often hold hundreds of individual securities and it is not possible or practical to evaluate each separate holding.

I have already indicated that I do not own open-end or exchange-traded funds. This is strictly because of yield – I have no other reason to avoid these funds and obviously there are millions of investors who disagree with me and are very happy to hold such investments. So even if my funds are all closed-end, I want to make clear that the model we will develop in this section can be applied to any type of fund.

Excluding ETFs, investment funds are structured and managed by investment professionals. It is simply in the nature of things that these people want to justify their positions and their salaries, and the only real way to do that is to trade. So it is not unusual to see annual portfolio turnover rates ranging from a low of perhaps 15-35% for preferred stock, bond, and utility funds to rates of 60-90% for healthcare and tech funds. In some cases these annual rates may be well in excess of 100%, indicating that, on average, no security is held for more than one year.

So the first thing we have to adjust to when considering investment funds is that we are not looking at anything resembling a buy and hold strategy. In 2010, the average holding duration for mutual funds and pension funds was only 1.5 years.[29] So we cannot expect to achieve consistent dividend

---

29   Cremers, Pareek, Sautner, "Stock Duration, Analysts Recommendations, and Misvaluation" December 2014.

growth as we do when holding a stable portfolio of individual securities. To the extent that we do experience "dividend" growth (higher distribution payments from the fund), these will come primarily from the trading successes of the managers – buying stocks at lower prices with higher yields, and then selling at higher prices when market yields fall.

Given this reality, I do not invest in funds with the expectation that I will see any significant increase in yield. Rather, I invest first to achieve an immediate yield that is significantly higher than straight equity investment, and secondly is very well protected by the total operating income of the fund.

Does this represent a retreat from our Dividend Growth philosophy? Well, yes, to a limited extent, it does. As I am retired, I need current income for support, and this is certainly a quick way to achieve that. But even younger investors might benefit from some exposure here to "jump start" cash flow and reinvestment opportunities. However, the key disadvantage is that without dependable distribution growth, fund yields will not keep up with inflation, and so I limit funds to 25% of my total portfolio.

So our selection model for investment funds will focus primarily on dividend/distribution yield and distribution coverage/protection, but will not include a metric for distribution growth. Instead we will focus on distribution *stability*. We are starting off with a strong yield, and while we may not expect it to grow, we do want to feel comfortable that it will not decline. Stability in distribution depends ultimately on performance, but we will also see that some funds adopt a fixed distribution policy, providing investors with a long-term consistent level payout that does not necessarily track current performance.

Sources of Investment Fund Distributions

Investment funds do not create a product or offer a service. Rather, they own the stock of other companies that do these things. So when analyzing investment funds, the first thing we have to adjust is our concept of "profit." Funds do not generate a "profit" in any active sense; rather, they receive passive income from their investments in two forms:

- *Net Investment Income (NII)*
  This consists of all dividend, distribution, and interest income received from the investment portfolio, less all management, administrative, and interest expenses. This is the "best" source of fund income, in that it is usually sustainable and reasonably predictable.

- *Capital Gains*
  These may be *realized* gains (the fund has sold the underlying security) or *unrealized* gains (increase in market price, subject to future fluctuation). This source of fund income may not be sustainable or predictable.

Adding together Net Investment Income (NII) and Capital Gains produces *Total Operating Income* (TOI). Some funds refer to this as *Net Increase in Net Assets* (NINA).

When you receive a distribution from a fund, the fund must *break that distribution down into three components.* This breakdown will appear on the 1099 form you receive from the fund at the end of the year. These components are:

- Net Investment Income: Taxed as ordinary income
- Realized Capital Gains: Short-term: taxed as ordinary income. Long-term: usually taxed at 15%.
- Return of Capital: Subject to income tax deferral (see Attachment D).

"Return of Capital" (ROC) is a tricky concept that deserves attention. When I see it, it waves a "yellow flag" at me that merits further investigation.

A Return of Capital distribution *does not come from earnings* – neither from Net Interest Income nor Realized Capital Gains. ROC means is that the fund is *distributing back to you part of your own capital* – the money that you invested when you bought your shares. This investment is reflected as "Paid in Capital" (PIC) on the fund balance sheet,[30] and when the fund pays out ROC, the PIC account is reduced.

Why would a fund make an ROC distribution? Well, in the first place, keep in mind that investment funds offering high distribution rates place a very high priority on maintaining a level (or increasing) distribution payout. This is what investors are attracted to and are counting on. Occasionally there will be periods of time when fund TOI/NINA will not be enough to cover the distribution. If that happens, rather than cut the distribution, the fund may cover the deficit through Return of Capital.

Secondly, for technical reasons there are occasions when a fund manager may wish to distribute *unrealized* capital gains. But he can't allocate such a distribution to either Net Investment Income or Realized Capital Gains – he must allocate this portion of the distribution to Return of Capital.

In the first case, the total distribution is higher than TOI/NINA. So in simplest terms, more money went out then came in. This means that the *Net Asset Value (NAV) or net worth of the fund declined*. This is an example of *destructive Return of Capital*.

In the second case, TOI/NINA may have been enough to cover the total distribution, including the ROC component. Again in simplest terms, more money came in then went out.

---

30   Technically, "Paid in Capital" represents the money contributed by the original shareholders. You "inherit" a position when you buy your shares.

This means that *Net Asset Value increased*. This is an example of *non-destructive Return of Capital*.

So the question to be addressed is: How serious is a destructive Return of Capital?

If ROC is used *occasionally* to maintain a distribution that is normally covered by TOI/NINA, then I have no problem with that. The fund manager is probably correct in using ROC to preserve a distribution, because a drop in distribution would send a bad signal to the market and share price would fall. So in this limited situation, some destructive return would be acceptable.

There is another rather limited situation in which destructive ROC may be OK. If the fund *is selling at a discount* (market price is below NAV), *and* if the shareholder is *participating in a DRIP* (Dividend Reinvestment Plan), then the shareholder benefits by reinvesting his distribution, because he is buying an interest in fund assets – securities – at a discount. If the fund is selling at a 20% discount, then the shareholder is taking $1.00 from the fund and turning around to acquire $1.25 of its assets.

The problem with destructive Return of Capital occurs when ROC is used frequently – or even continuously – to fund distributions that are not supported by income or gains. This confuses investors who believe that a fund is healthy simply because they are getting a big check. But if destructive ROC is used extensively, then the size of the fund must continue to shrink as securities must be sold to cover the distributions. This reduces the asset base, in turn reducing TOI/NINA, and requiring more ROC. Carried to its logical conclusion, the fund would literally disappear, or could only survive with a drastic reduction in the distribution.

To illustrate what can go wrong with ROC, I would like to introduce you to what I consider to be the worst closed end fund I have ever reviewed – *Cornerstone Total Return (CRF)* – a "perfect storm" of shareholder disaster. Here is a five-year review of per share fund performance:

FYE DECEMBER 31

	2014	2013	2012	2011	2010
Net Asset Value – Open	$20.56	20.36	21.88	26.60	28.76
Net Investment Income	0.16	0.24	0.20	0.08	0.00
Capital Gain (Loss)	2.15	3.76	2.48	0.20	2.72
NINA/TOI	2.31	4.00	2.68	0.28	2.72
Distributions:					
From Net Investment Income:	(0.16)	(0.92)	(1.24)	(0.08)	—
From Realized Cap Gain:	(0.82)	(0.80)	—	—	—
From Return of Capital:	(3.20)	(2.64)	(3.44)	(5.28)	(5.84)
Total Distributions:	(4.18)	(4.36)	(4.68)	(5.36)	(5.84)
New Capital Raised:	—	0.56	0.48	0.36	0.96
Net Asset Value – Close	18.69	20.56	20.36	21.88	26.60
Return of Capital/ Distributions	76.6%	60.6%	73.5%	98.5%	100.0%

(Note that this is the basic five-year format that you will find in the financial statement of any investment fund. It provides much of the data you will need to analyze a fund for possible purchase).

Cornerstone has adopted a Managed Distribution Plan (fixed distribution payment) in which they are currently paying out an annual distribution that equals 21% of the fund's Net Asset Value. That is not a typo – TWENTY ONE PERCENT. This amount is just incredible – *the fund – which does not use leverage – would have to earn a return of 21% on its assets to avoid using destructive return of capital.* Such a return is impossible to achieve on any kind of consistent basis. And so to pay for distributions, the fund has used destructive ROC for this entire period. *Net Asset Value of the fund has declined 35% from $28.76 to $18.69!*

You will also notice that the fund has *reduced distributions every year* as well, from $5.84 to $4.18, a decrease of 28.4%. But even this steady distribution decline has not come close to eliminating the need for destructive ROC, which continues to shrink NAV at a much faster rate.

And here is another nice little trick. Recognizing the obvious fact that their fund is disappearing – and with it their fees – management has repeatedly raised more capital through rights offerings in four of the last five years (see italics above). Shareholders were given the "right" to buy more shares, the funds of which will no doubt be returned to them shortly – less the management fees assessed in the interim!

And to add further insult to injury, let's take a look at the market price of this fund. The fund achieved a high price of $156.96 at end of December 2006. Exactly one year later, December 2007, the price was $78.40, a drop of exactly 50%. One year after that, December 2008, the price was $30.40, fully 80% below the high price two years earlier. Today the price is $18.76, which represents a total price decline of 88% over the past nine years.

And here is perhaps the craziest thing of all. The fund tells its shareholders – clearly and in writing – exactly what it is doing and what it intends to continue doing. The offering circular specifically states that any funds raised through a rights offering may be returned to the shareholder! There is no attempt to evade this disclosure! But shareholders obviously don't understand this disclosure or else choose to ignore it. They are making the mistake of *confusing distribution yield with earnings yield*, and with Cornerstone, that is one colossal mistake!

So as I say, when I see Return of Capital, that raises a yellow flag which requires more investigation. I would just rather not see it, as it is a nuisance to be dealt with. In the majority of cases it is acceptable, but there are exceptions! So make sure you know the three components of a distribution, and look carefully to see whether Net Asset Value is increasing (without new stock offerings) or decreasing.

Metrics for Analyzing Investment Funds

I. *Distribution Yield*

Distribution Yield

Definition: Current distribution dollar amount projected over the next 12 months / Current fund price

Comment: Investment funds do not behave like corporations in that they do not increase distributions in any predictable manner. Distributions tend to be readjusted to reflect current performance. The exceptions are funds that establish a *Managed Distribution Plan (MDP)* under which distributions are held constant. As with stocks, we are calculating the projected distributions over the next twelve months, not the past year. Note that investment funds are more likely to pay distributions monthly.

Source: Morningstar "Quote" (first page) for the fund. Latest distribution shown at the bottom left. Price shown at top left.

II. *Distribution Protection*

Distribution Coverage

Unlike stocks, I make *two separate calculations of distribution coverage* for funds. The first calculation measures Total Operating Income (TOI) coverage, which includes both Net Interest Income (NII) and realized capital gains. However, capital gains are not as predictable as NII, and so I make a second calculation measuring the distribution coverage provided by *Net Interest Income (NII) only*. I consider this as a secondary but stronger source of distribution coverage.

Total Operating Income (TOI) Distribution Coverage

Definition: Four Years Weighted (5-4-3-2) Average: Total Operating Income (TOI) / Distributions

Comment: This ratio considers *all* sources of distribution coverage, including capital gains.

Source: See fund's annual or semiannual report for this data (See Morningstar "filings"). Find the five-year per share summary (example, page 176) found near the end of the report.

Net Investment Income (NII) Distribution Coverage
Definition: Last Four Years Weighted (5-4-3-2) Average: Net Investment Income (NII) / Distributions

Comment: A more conservative approach to distribution coverage that eliminates capital gains

Source: Same as TOI coverage / preceding paragraph

Net Asset Value Coverage
Definition: Most recent Net Asset Value (NAV) / Paid in Capital

Comment: This is a quick and effective way to measure the success of fund management since the inception of the fund. "Paid in Capital" is the amount initially invested in the fund. "Net Asset Value" measures the current net worth of the fund, which is equal to the original Paid in Capital plus (or minus) the accumulated gains (or losses) the fund has achieved since inception *after the payment of distributions.* If this ratio is 1.00, then management has just covered cumulative distributions with earnings. If the ratio is greater than 1.00, then management has more than covered distributions, in effect retaining some reserve. If the ratio is less than 1.00, then management has not covered distributions, and a cumulative deficit has been created. Obviously the higher the ratio, the better.[31]

---

31   If the fund has had one or more stock offerings since inception, that will initially increase both Net Asset Value and Paid in Capital in equal amounts. That will have the effect of improving a poor ratio (below 1.00) and reducing a good ratio (above 1.00). But unless the secondary offerings are quite large, the effect should be relatively minor. Also, be aware that the extensive use of destructive Return of Capital reduces both Paid in Capital

Source: Annual or Semiannual Report, "Statement of Assets and Liabilities" (bottom of statement)

Distribution History

Definition: Distribution History is determined by observing the number and the percentage of distribution cuts over the past ten years.

Comment: We are focusing here on the *stability of dividend payments*. We review the annual distribution payments over the past ten years, noting the number of times that the distribution was cut by more than 10%. We then calculate the percentage decrease between highest and lowest distribution payments over the past ten years. We assign a weight of 100 (out of 1000) to this metric, and the score is determined by the grid below.

Source: Longrundata.com. Select any start date within the last year just to generate a calculation. Distribution payments are shown below the return calculation.

	HIGH-LOW DISTRIBUTION DROP					
	0-10%	10-19%	20-29%	30-39%	40-49%	50-59%
# DISTRIBUTION CUTS OVER 10%						
0	100	95	90	80	60	40
1		90	80	70	55	40
2		80	70	60	45	30
3		65	55	45	30	20

Leverage

Definition: Total Borrowed Funds / Total Assets

Comment: As we have discussed, closed-end funds employ leverage to boost earnings. However, this increases risk. Therefore we

---

as well as Net Asset Value, creating a ratio that may not look as bad as the situation truly warrants. So this metric will be compromised in that case.

consider leverage to be a negative factor in our selection screen.

Source: Morningstar "Quote" (first page) of the fund. Leverage is listed at the top right of the page.

III: Performance

Weighted Average Total Return

Definition: Sum of all distributions and price appreciation generated within a given period of time.

Comment: We average the total return of the fund for periods of three years, five years, and ten years. We apply weights of 3, 2, and 1 to the returns for 10 years, 5 years, and 3 years respectively.

Source: Morningstar "Performance" tab. Trailing Total Returns (Price) is shown midway down page.

Ten Year Total Return Standard Deviation

Definition: Standard Deviation measures the variability of sample values around the mean (average) of that sample. We calculate the STDEV of all ten total return values for each of the past ten years.

Comment: A lower standard deviation means that the sample values cluster more closely around the mean, and that investors should therefore expect less volatility. There is some argument as to whether volatility per se is synonymous with the concept of risk. But whatever the definition of risk may be, every investor would prefer that his portfolio behave in a stable, steady, non-volatile fashion.

Source: Morningstar "Performance" tab (Second graph / "Annual Returns")

Net Asset Value Growth Rate

Definition: Net Asset Value: Five Year Weighted Average Growth Rate

Comment: We want to see how the fund has performed over the last five years in terms of building the net worth of the fund. In effect this is a measure of profitability and profit retention.

Source: Annual or Semiannual Fund Report. See five-year per share summary near the end of the report.

Recession Recovery Index
Definition: As explained in Section III.

Preliminary Fund Selection Screen

As we did with individual securities – corporations and partnerships – we will subject investment funds to two screens. The preliminary screen consists of six metrics which will eliminate the great majority of funds from further consideration. For those funds that pass the preliminary screen, the final screen will be applied to rank funds for possible purchase.

Yield: The fund should have a minimum current distribution yield of 5.00%.

If we are going to sacrifice distribution growth, then I want to start with a yield that is substantially above normal equity yields. This start rate will eliminate the great majority of mutual and ETF securities, so this rate may be too steep for investors who are attracted to those funds.

Distribution Coverage: 4-Year Weighted Average TOI / Distributions ratio should be greater than 1.00

The fund does not have to cover its distribution every year, but should cover over the past four years.

Net Asset Value Coverage: Ratio NAV/Paid in Capital should not be lower than .90.

I will accept a minimum ratio just below 1.00, meaning that, since inception, the fund has not quite covered its distributions through net investment income and capital gains. But this will at least show me that any substantial damage from 2007 or 2008 had been largely repaired. Note: If there is extensive use of destructive capital, do not use this ratio as a screen metric.

Distribution History:No more than 2 distribution cuts over 10% during the last 10 years.

Weighted Average Total Return: Weighted Average Total Return (3-5-10 years) above 7.5%

This implies that in addition to a minimum yield of 5%, we expect price appreciation of at least 2.5%.

Current Market Price: Must be greater than 75% of the pre-2008 high market price.

When you look a fund's price history, *make sure you go back at least ten years*. I am constantly amazed by the number of CEFs I have reviewed that have a decent record of price appreciation since 2009, but if you back up another year or two, these funds completely collapsed, with price drops in 2007 and 2008 of 70% or more, far greater than the general market contraction at that time. Many – such as Cornerstone Total Return – have never recovered from these steep losses. Such losses may have been due to margin calls made by lenders as prices collapsed, requiring forced sales of securities in 2007-2008.

Cheating:

As was the case with individual securities, I permit myself to waive one – and only one – default on the seven metrics listed above. Two defaults mean elimination.

Finding Funds to Screen:

The Closed End Fund Association is a national trade association representing the closed-end fund industry. Their website, cefa.com, offers an extensive listing of CEFs broken down by various asset classes, including Domestic Equities, Global Equities, Fixed Income, and Municipal Bonds.

Final Fund Selection Screen

As we did with corporations and partnerships in Section Three, we will set up a quantitative model to evaluate investment funds with a total (perfect) score of 1000. We will include ten metrics in this screen, the same number that we used in evaluating individual securities, *although we will stress distribution stability rather than distribution growth.* Each of these ten metrics will be given a weight, which will represent that portion of the total score allocated to that metric. We assign these weights to reflect the relative importance we attribute to each metric.

Also as we did in Section Three, we will determine certain multipliers and dividers in order to convert metric data into a screen score. This is largely a trial-and-error process in which we try to reward superior results without unduly penalizing satisfactory performance.

The table below shows the metrics selected, the multiplier/divider for that metric, and the maximum score permitted (weight). The "cut off data value" is the data value which produces the maximum score, such that any higher (better) data value will not increase the screen score. If the score resulting from the data value and the multiplier/divider exceeds the maximum, then the maximum score will apply.

Note that the Leverage metric does not use a multiplier/divider. Rather, the leverage percent is deducted from 45 to determine the score.

Metric	Multiplier/ Divider	Maximum Score	Cut Off Data Value
Distribution Yield:	28X	250	8.93%
TOI Distribution Coverage	100X	200	2.00
NII Distribution Coverage	100X	100	1.00
NAV/Paid in Capital	50X	75	1.50
Distribution History	grid (page 180)	100	0 Cuts
Leverage (%)	45–L	40	45%
3-5-10 Yr Wt Ave Total Return (%)	7X	80	11.4%
Total Return STDEV (%)	480/	40	12.0%
NAV 5 Yr Wt Ave Growth Rate (%)	25X	75	3.0%
Recession Recovery	24,000/	40 / 1000	600

We will now offer two case studies to show how the final screen works in practice. Both funds have passed the preliminary screen with no defaults.

Case Study #1: DNP SELECT INCOME (DNP)

DNP Select Income is a well established CEF originally launched in 1987. The fund invests in infrastructure companies including utilities (57%), energy (26%), and telecoms (14%). The fund has offered a Managed Distribution Plan and has paid a distribution of $.065 every month for over 18 years. Screen metrics are solid, as shown below:

Metric	Metric Value	Mutiplier/ Divider	Maximum	Final Score
Distribution Yield:	7.69%	28	250	215
TOI Distribution Coverage:	1.69	100	200	169
NII Distribution coverage:	.43	100	100	43
NAV/Paid in Capital:	1.39	50	75	70
Distribution History:	0 cuts	from chart- page 180	100	100
Leverage:	30.2%	45-L	40	15
Wt. Ave. Total Return:	7.6%	7	80	53
Total Return STDEV:	25.29	480/	40	19
NAV Growth Rate:	4.42%	25X	75	75
Recession Recovery:	987	24,000/	40	24
			1000	**783**

DNP's Managed Distribution Plan has produced a rock steady payout since 1997, earning a maximum score for Distribution History. Equally important, the fund has been able to pay this distribution while achieving a TOI distribution coverage ratio of 1.69 over the last four years. NAV/Paid in Capital is also very solid, indicating a long term positive retention of income after distributions. DNP also exceeds the maximum score for the NAV Growth Rate. This is a very strong score and I would consider this fund for purchase.

Case Study #2: Main Street Capital Corporation (MAIN)

Main Street Capital Corporation is a CEF Business Development Company formed in 2006. The company is internally managed (does not retain an outside investment advisor) and consequently has one of the lowest expense ratios in its industry. The company is highly regarded and trades at a consistent premium to NAV because of steady performance and a solid portfolio.

Metric	Metric Value	Mutiplier/ Divider	Maximum	Final Score
Distribution Yield:	7.48%	28	250	209
TOI Distribution Coverage:	1.18	100	200	118
NII Distribution Coverage:	.91	100	100	91
NAV/Paid in Capital:	1.10	50	75	55
Distribution History:	1 cut/11% drop	from chart page 180	100	90
Leverage:	37.8%	45–L	40	7
Wt. Ave. Total Return:	16.9%	7	80	80
Total Return STDEV:	30.44	480/	40	16
NAV Growth Rate:	12.1%	25X	75	75
Recession Recovery:	391	24,000/	40	40
			1000	**781**

This is a young company off to a strong start. It has a solid yield, fair TOI coverage, and excellent NII coverage. It shines in the performance metrics of total return, NAV growth, and recession recovery. Also note that the company has a high ratio of insider ownership, always a good sign. I would consider this fund for purchase.

Diversification

When you buy an investment fund, you are buying into a portfolio of dozens or hundreds of individual securities, so micro diversification is already addressed and not an issue. However, macro diversification still is. Most funds specialize in a certain industrial sector or a certain asset class, so you will still have to monitor and balance your exposure in these areas. Again I would recommend Morningstar Portfolio Manager with its "X-Ray" screen that will break down the fund by its individual holdings and allocate each holding to the proper diversification category.

Summary: Section Four

If an investment fund is managed, the fund will be involved in active – and perhaps very active – trading. If the fund is an ETF, there may be no active management but the holdings of the fund are nevertheless subject to frequent shifts in the composition of the fund index.

In either case, investment funds do not offer anything like a "buy and hold" strategy and therefore an investor cannot expect to achieve the gradual and predictable distribution growth that we have defined as our primary goal. Instead, some funds – particularly closed end funds that can employ leverage – can offer very attractive yields at the time of purchase. This means that fund distribution, while hopefully high, steady, and predictable, cannot be expected to keep up with inflation. So while you may start off with a very attractive distribution yield of 5% or more, after perhaps ten years this yield may not look quite as attractive relative to an individual security with strong dividend growth. This is why I think that investment funds are better suited for retirees than for younger investors. In either case, I would not commit the bulk of my portfolio to investment funds and I personally limit my fund ownership to 25% of my portfolio.

The last two sections have addressed *how* to construct a dividend growth portfolio – an organic portfolio that will supply the investor with a steady stream of rising income. *The ultimate goal is to become 100% organic,* meaning that your portfolio income – along with other sources of income – *will be able to fund all of your living expenses in retirement* and also cover inflationary increases in these expenses. If you can achieve this goal, then *you should never have to sell a share.*

You will be in control of your investments –
not the other way around.

We now turn to the last of our four questions – *when* do we buy? We have selected some great securities to fill our portfolio, but how do we know that we are getting a good or fair price for a security at the point of purchase? The dividends/distributions look very attractive, but what are they actually worth to us today, and *is that value – that worth – in proper alignment with the current price?*

SECTION FIVE

WHEN

Be fearful when others are greedy.

Be greedy when others are fearful.

— *Warren Buffett*

What This Section Will Cover

At this point we will assume that you have screened a number of securities through our protocol and you have selected those that you wish to buy. So the final question is:

Is this the right time to buy?
Is the price listed today a fair price to pay for this stock?
Will I achieve my expected rate of return?

What is the intrinsic fair value of this security today?

There are two basic schools of thought regarding stock pricing and valuation. The most recent technique to emerge is known as *Modern Portfolio Theory (MPT)*, which became popular in the 1950's and is still widely accepted by money managers today. This theory is based on two fundamental assumptions. First, all knowledge that exists about a particular stock is instantly known to all investors everywhere, so you can't gain any advantage by learning and knowing something before others know it. Second, investors act rationally – they act carefully to avoid risk without adequate return – at all times. Emotions such as fear, greed, panic – even stupidity – simply do not enter into the investment decision.

Given these two assumptions, MPT concludes that securities pricing is *perfectly efficient*. Stock prices adjust instantly based on universal, equal knowledge between all investors, and these prices are determined in a rational manner after that knowledge is processed. So you simply can't "beat the market" – you can't gain the upper hand – and it is pointless to try. *The market value of a stock always equals its fair value.* The timing of your transaction is irrelevant. In fact, the selection of individual stocks is irrelevant. Your only real option is to buy a number of low-cost, unmanaged index funds, widely diversified by market capitalization, industry, and geography.

The second school could be called the *Value School*. This is the approach first derived by Benjamin Graham in the 1930's and now practiced by numerous major investors, most notably Warren Buffett. The basic idea is that through meticulous study and analysis, *you can derive a fair value for a company that may not – and probably won't – be equal to the market value. Intrinsic fair value and market value are two very different things.* Markets are not 100% efficient and investors are by no means rational. Therefore it is indeed possible to buy a company for less than its fair value, and in fact it is important to achieve a "margin of safety" between fair value (true worth) and market value (cost) when you buy.

I studied Modern Portfolio Theory in graduate school and I must say that there are some really cool graphs with lines labeled "efficient frontier" that bend backwards and hit something called a "tangency portfolio." All very interesting intellectual theory. But ultimately to me that's just what it is – theory.

I look at market behavior and I just *know* that what I see is neither efficient nor rational. I am sure some academicians might overwhelm me with their "proofs," but I am definitely going to side with ol' Ben Graham and Warren Buffett on this one!

So we will look at a number of popular methods used to determine the value or worth of a company's stock. Certain methods value a stock relative to other stocks; other methods value a stock relative to its own past performance. A third approach involves some form of discounted cash flow analysis. Hopefully by using some – or even all – of these approaches, you will be able to determine a fair value for a company, compare it to the market price, establish a margin of safety, and start your portfolio!

When to Buy

Price/Earnings Ratio

The first method used to establish the fair value of a company's stock is to consider its price/earnings ratio. This is simply the price per share today divided by the most recent annual earnings per share figure. In effect this ratio tells you how many years it will take to recover your investment in a stock. If a company has a P/E ratio of 15, then it will take fifteen years of today's earnings to recover your initial investment price.

Some analysts like to calculate a *forward* P/E ratio. Instead of using current earnings from the *last* 12 months, they use projected earnings for the *next* 12 months. Since projected earnings are almost always higher than current earnings, the forward P/E almost always makes the stock look less expensive (more reasonably priced) than the current P/E ratio. As this whole forward calculation is based on projection rather than fact, I prefer to stick with the current P/E ratio in my analysis.

There are two ways to use the P/E ratio to determine a stock's value. The first way is to *determine value relative to other stocks*. In this case you would compare the P/E ratio of any given stock to some market benchmark. For example, the current P/E ratio of the S&P 500 is 19.6. One could calculate a "relative" P/E ratio for any stock by dividing that stock's P/E by the S&P P/E of 19.6. If the relative P/E is above 1.00, that stock would be considered "expensive" compared to the S&P 500 average (it would take longer than 19.6 years to earn your money back). If the relative P/E is below 1.00, then the stock would be considered less expensive than average. The greater the relative P/E amount differs from 1.00, the greater the degree of over- or undervaluation.

The second approach to using the P/E ratio is to *determine value relative to the stock itself*. To do this, you *compare a company's current P/E ratio to its average P/E ratio for the past five years*. (Morningstar provides this data under the "valuation" tab). If the current P/E ratio is significantly below the average, this may indicate that the stock is undervalued. If the current P/E is significantly above the average, then the reverse is true and the stock is overvalued.

A slight refinement here would be to calculate the percentage difference between the current and average values. A small percentage difference would not be of much interest, but a large difference would indicate that an over- or undervalued situation might exist.

As an example, looking at our case study Emerson Electric (EMR), we see a current P/E of 12.1 and a five year average P/E of 20.2. The percentage difference shows the current P/E to be 40% under its average, certainly a very large spread. This tends to confirm my feeling that this stock is undervalued, as our previous review concluded.

A further refinement would be to expand this current vs. average approach to other performance ratios, such as current dividend yield vs. 5-year average dividend yield, or current price/cash flow vs. 5-year average price/cash flow. If all of these ratios show a similar over- or undervalued condition, then you would have a higher level of confidence in reaching a value judgment.

The P/E ratio is a quick and popular way of valuing a stock, but it is limited in its usefulness:

- The P/E ratio varies dramatically between industries. A utility might have a P/E ratio of 10 while a technology company might have a P/E well over 40 (Amazon today has a P/E of 91). So comparing P/E ratios is only relevant if you are comparing companies in the same industry.

- The P/E ratio is a stagnant number that does not consider future growth. A high P/E may certainly be reasonable and warranted for a company experiencing rapid growth. Tech companies have high P/E ratios precisely for this reason.
- For a dividend growth investor, this ratio is of virtually no value at all for the simple reason that it focuses strictly on earnings and gives no consideration whatsoever to cash dividends.

PEG Ratio

An improvement on the P/E ratio is a calculation known as the PEG ratio, or Price Earnings Growth Ratio. *This ratio is calculated by dividing the P/E ratio by the estimated Earnings Growth Rate.*

PEG = P/E RATIO ÷ EARNINGS GROWTH RATE

This ratio therefore takes future earnings growth into account. An example would be:

Slow Growth Company A has a P/E ratio of 8. The company's earnings are expected to grow 8% per year. Therefore the PEG ratio is 8 ÷ 8 = 1.

Fast Grow Company B has a P/E ratio of 24. Its earnings are expected to grow 24% per year. Therefore the PEG ratio is 24 ÷ 24 = 1.

So the PEG ratio is the same for both companies. Both companies have the *same relative value* in that you are paying three times as much for the earnings of Company B but that is offset by the fact that earnings will grow three times faster than Company A. *So looking only at price, earnings, and earnings growth, you should be ambivalent as to which company you might wish to buy.*

So the PEG ratio gives us two improvements over the P/E ratio. First, it takes earnings growth into account. Second, it is a relative metric that lets us compare stocks belonging to different industries.

The argument is made that in a truly efficient market, every stock would have a PEG ratio of 1.0, wherein the P/E ratio was an exact reflection of earnings growth. Of course the market is not always efficient – certainly not in the short term, and estimates of future earnings growth can be wildly divergent, as we have already discussed. So given an inefficient market, the argument says that a stock with a *PEG ratio below 1.0 is undervalued,* since its price does not reflect its earnings growth potential. Similarly, a stock with a *PEG ratio over 1.0 is overvalued,* as the price is above earnings potential.

I can't resist an interesting example here. As mentioned above, Amazon has a P/E ratio today of 91. Yet analysts project earnings will grow at a rate of 98% over the next 5 years! So the PEG ratio is 0.9. This means that Amazon is a bargain! (A bargain, that is, if you are comfortable with a 98% growth rate!)

Dividend Adjusted PEG Ratio

The PEG ratio, like the P/E ratio, is of little practical value to dividend investors since the focus is entirely on earnings. However, the formula can be modified for dividend investors by *adding the dividend yield to the denominator.* The formula for the *Dividend Adjusted PEG – PEG (DA) –* now becomes:

PEG (DA) = P/E Ratio ÷ (Earnings Growth Rate + Dividend Yield)

As an example, consider our case study Emerson Electric (EMR):

P/E Ratio: 12.1%
Earnings Growth: 7.7%
Dividend Yield: 4.4%

The calculation of PEG is: 12.1 ÷ 7.7 = 1.57
The calculation of PEG (DA) is:12.1 ÷ (7.7 + 4.4) = 12.1 ÷ 12.1 = 1.00

So the inclusion of the dividend yield shows that the stock has – by this standard – a fair value.

Enterprise Value Ratio

Although it is not well known, I think that the Enterprise Value Ratio is an interesting way to estimate fair value. The idea is to develop a number that represents the market purchase price you would have to pay today to buy an entire company. You then divide that number by the annual cash flow generated by the company to determine how many years of cash flow it would take to pay the purchase price.

This ratio is similar in concept to the P/E ratio, but more comprehensive in that it considers: 1) The entire capitalization of the company, instead of just common stock, and 2) cash flow instead of just earnings.

ENTERPRISE VALUE = MARKET VALUE OF (COMMON STOCK + PREFERRED STOCK + DEBT) – CASH

EBITDA = EARNINGS BEFORE INTEREST, TAXES, DEPRECIATION, AND AMORTIZATION

ENTERPRISE VALUE RATIO = ENTERPRISE VALUE ÷ EBITDA

So if you were to buy a company, you would theoretically have to pay off all the common stockholders and all the preferred stockholders (if any), as well as debt holders. However, you could use the company cash to reduce this purchase price. You would look at EBITDA (one common method of measuring cash flow) to determine how many years it would take to recover your investment. Obviously the lower the ratio, the better – a low ratio might indicate a company that is undervalued, just as a low P/E would.

As stated, Enterprise Value is very difficult to calculate as the market value of debt may not be known. I would just use the book value of debt as the best estimate. However, you can find this ratio already calculated at finance.yahoo.com. Enter the company symbol at the top, then hit "Key Statistics" twice. The calculation appears at the bottom of the first column.

Dividend Discount Model

Instead of focusing on earnings, there are models that determine stock value *strictly by the cash dividends that are paid*. A very simple dividend model has only two variables: the dividend projected for the next year and the return that the investor requires for that stock. Therefore:

$$\text{VALUE} = \text{DIVIDEND/REQUIRED RETURN}$$

So if you want a yield of 5% on a stock that pays an annual dividend of $1.50, you would be willing to pay $1.50 / .05 = $ 30.00 for that stock. If the current price is below $30.00, the stock is "cheap." If the price is above $30.00, the stock is "expensive."

This simple equation does not include dividend growth. So a modification of the model is as follows:

$$\text{VALUE} = \text{DIVIDEND} \div \text{REQUIRED RETURN} - \text{DIVIDEND GROWTH}$$

This is the basic Dividend Discount Model, also known as the Gordon Model for the academician who developed it. An example would be:

Company A (Stable): Dividend of $1.50 – Projected dividend growth of 3.5% – Required Return 7.5%

(7.5% Required Return is relatively low, but might be appropriate for a stable, non-cyclical company)

VALUE = $1.50 / (.075 - .035) = $1.50 / .04 = $ 37.50

<u>Company B</u> (Volatile): Dividend of $1.50 – Projected dividend growth of 6% – Required Return 10%

(10% Required Return is higher, given the volatility of company earnings)

VALUE = $1.50 / (.10 - .06) = $1.50 / .04 = $ 37.50

You would be willing to pay the same amount for both stocks. The relative safety of the first company (lower required return) compensates for the faster dividend growth of the second.

But we again face some serious limitations when using this model:

- This formula assumes a constant rate of dividend growth. This assumption may be reasonably accurate for older, mature companies but it is certainly not true for the great majority of firms.
- The formula is based on holding a stock in perpetuity. This may not be a poor assumption for a "buy and hold" investor but is obviously flawed for shorter-term investors.
- As the required return and the dividend growth rate come closer together, the value may become unrealistically high.
- The model will not work at all if the dividend growth rate exceeds the required return. This produces a negative denominator and the calculation becomes meaningless.

Advanced Dividend Discount Model

An improvement on this model *allows the dividend growth rate to change.* Such a model can be found on *moneychimp.com.* Hit the yellow field to determine stock value. On the right hand side, hit "DCF Calculator." This model is set up to discount Earnings per Share, but you can simply substitute the anticipated 12-month Dividend Per Share amount for EPS. You enter your required return (I use 8.5%), an initial growth rate, and then a second growth rate after 5 years. The model then makes a calculation of value. I use this model to determine a fair value for every stock I consider. It is not the only approach to value I use, but it helps me *focus on the importance of discounting dividend cash flow (real cash) rather than discounting earnings.*

Non-Perpetuity Discount Model

All of the models discussed above assume that *securities are held in perpetuity – they are never sold.* This assumption might not seem objectionable to a long-term investor, since the discounted value of a sale in the remote future might have a relatively small effect on today's value. However, in reality there are very few true long-term "buy and hold" investors. In 2010, the holding duration for America's core stockholder class – mutual funds and pension funds – was only 1.5 years.[32] So in order for our valuation methods to more closely reflect reality, I think it would be instructive to assume *that stocks are held for some finite period.*

I am going to make the assumption that stocks are held for a period of 15 years and then sold.

This is purely arbitrary on my part, and far longer than the average holding period. But I think that Dividend Growth Investors ought to establish a long-term investment horizon during which compound interest will work most effectively.

So in order to create a non-perpetuity discount model, we are going to project out dividend payments into the future for 15 years. After 15 years we will also sell the stock for some final principal value.

Our question therefore is: What is this cash flow stream worth to us today? *What is its present value?*

---

32   Cremers, Pareek, Sautner, "Stock Duration, Analysts Recommendations, and Misvaluation" December 2014.

Here is the basic idea of what "present value" means. We would intuitively prefer to have someone give us a dollar today rather than in five years. But why do we feel that way – in logical terms? The reason is that if we had one dollar today, we could invest it and watch its value increase every year for five years. At the end of five years, it would be worth more than one dollar. How much more would of course depend on the rate of interest we could get on our investment.

So if one dollar today is worth more than one dollar tomorrow, then the reverse is also true – one dollar tomorrow is worth less than one dollar today. *How much less depends on the earnings rate – the discount rate – that we wish to achieve on this investment.*

The question of discount rate deserves some discussion. We have seen that over extended periods of time, the market returns a *real* (inflation adjusted) return of 6.5%. So when we consider the *absolute* rate we want to achieve in the market, we would add an estimate for inflation to this 6.5% number. Inflation today is extremely low, and in some countries we are actually seeing *deflation* occur. However, most economic forecasts for the United States today use an inflation number of 2.0-2.5%.

So *this would produce a discount rate of 8.5-9.0%.* For a very stable, non-cyclical stock, we might feel comfortable with a lower earnings (discount) rate of perhaps 7.5%. For a volatile, cyclical stock, we might require a higher rate, perhaps 10-11%. But in general I feel comfortable with a discount rate of 8.5% for most of the established stocks that would pass our screens with a high score.

So our non-perpetuity model will calculate net present value using a discount rate of 8.5%.

Now we have to make an assumption as to the final value of our stock when we sell it. Here some history may help us.

I reviewed the S&P 500 opening (January 1) average for each of the past 100 years. Since we are looking at an investment period of 15 years, I studied every discrete 15-year period over the past century to compare the opening average and the closing average. I found that you have to go back 85 years to January 1930 to find the last 15 year period (1930 – 1945) when the opening S&P average was higher than the closing average. *So for every discrete 15-year period since 1930, an investor in the S&P 500 would have gotten his entire original principal back, and achieved some level of capital gain.*

Looking at all 15-year periods for the past 65 years, I found that *the lowest S&P return for any 15-year period since 1950 was a 26% gain* (1960-1975). So I believe that it is quite reasonable and conservative to assume that we can achieve a capital gain of at least 25% on our investment.

Further, *there are only nine 15-year periods since 1950 (13.6% out of 66 such periods) when the return on the S&P 500 was less than 50%.* So a slightly less conservative assumption would be that we could achieve a 50% return on our original investment.

We need one more consideration to construct our model. The dividend discount model presented above assumed a constant dividend growth rate in perpetuity. We have addressed the issue of perpetuity and we will also address the issue of dividend growth. We will calculate net present value assuming no change in dividend growth for 15 years, but *we will also calculate net present value assuming slower rates of dividend growth in later years.*

The tables below show the net present value today of a stock that pays an annual dividend of $1.00. This is what you would pay today for this stock, *given a 15-year holding period and an 8.5% discount rate.* The first table assumes a 25% capital gain on the sale, and the second table assumes a 50% gain. Each table shows initial dividend growth rates ranging from 0% - 10% for the first seven years, and subsequent eight year growth rates that are equal to or less than these initial rates.

FAIR VALUE OF A STOCK WITH A CURRENT DIVIDEND OF $1.00

DIVIDENDS TERMINATE AFTER 15 YEARS

DISCOUNT RATE: 8.5%

TABLE A

STOCK SOLD IN YEAR 16 FOR 125% OF INITIAL COST

	DIVIDEND GROWTH RATE FOR FIRST SEVEN YEARS									
	0%	2%	3%	4%	5%	6%	7%	8%	9%	10%
After Seven Years										
Dividend Growth Is Unchanged	12.56	14.34	15.34	16.44	17.63	18.93	20.33	21.86	23.54	25.37
Dividend Growth Reduced 25%	12.56	14.21	15.15	16.14	17.21	18.37	19.64	20.96	22.40	23.97
Dividend Growth Reduced 50%	12.56	14.10	14.95	15.85	16.81	17.84	18.95	20.12	21.38	22.72
No Further Dividend Growth	12.56	13.87	14.57	15.31	16.08	16.90	17.76	18.65	19.59	20.58

Most Conservative Valuation

Most Optimistic Valuation

FAIR VALUE OF A STOCK WITH A CURRENT DIVIDEND OF $1.00

DIVIDENDS TERMINATE AFTER 15 YEARS

DISCOUNT RATE: 8.5%

TABLE B

STOCK SOLD IN YEAR 16 FOR 150% OF INITIAL COST

	DIVIDEND GROWTH RATE FOR FIRST SEVEN YEARS									
	0%	2%	3%	4%	5%	6%	7%	8%	9%	10%
After Seven Years										
Dividend Growth Is Unchanged	14.00	15.98	17.10	18.31	19.64	21.08	22.65	24.36	26.23	28.27
Dividend Growth Reduced 25%	14.00	15.84	16.88	17.99	19.17	20.47	21.86	23.34	24.96	26.71
Dividend Growth Reduced 50%	14.00	15.70	16.66	17.66	18.74	19.88	21.12	22.42	23.82	25.31
No Further Dividend Growth	14.00	15.45	16.24	17.06	17.92	18.83	19.79	20.78	21.83	22.93

Most Conservative Valuation

Most Optimistic Valuation

EXAMPLES:

Company A pays a dividend of $2.36. Dividend growth is projected at 6% for the first seven years and then drops 50% to 3% for the last eight years. What is the present value of the stock (fair price) if we assume a 50% capital gain on the sale?

Answer: Table B: 6% dividend growth (reduced 50%): 19.88 X 2.36 = $ 46.92

Company B pays a dividend of $1.76. Dividend growth is projected at 4.5% for the first seven years and then drops 25% to 3.375% for the last eight years. What is the present value of the stock if we assume a 50% capital gain on the sale?

Answer: Table B: We take the average between 4% and 5% dividend growth (reduced 25%):

$17.99 + 19.17/2 = $18.58. $18.58 X 1.76 = $32.70.

I should point out that even the "most optimistic" scenario highlighted above is still a very conservative approach to valuation. Keep in mind that we have limited capital gains in that model to just 50% over the course of 15 years. That equates to a growth rate of stock value of just 2.7% per year, historically a very modest amount. Recall also that of the 66 15-year periods since 1950, fully 86.4% of such periods produced a capital gain in excess of 50%.

So don't be surprised if most of the stocks you evaluate have a current price that exceeds the values calculated from the tables presented above. Nevertheless, this model is likely to find some interesting values, if consistently applied. Here are some current examples (October 2015):

Company	Annual Dividend	Dividend Growth	Current Price	Most Optimistic Valuation	Most Conservative Valuation
Royal Dutch Shell (B)	$3.76	2.0%	$55.60	$60.08	$52.15
TELUS Corp	1.28	10.0%	33.21	36.18	26.34
Collectors Universe	1.40	0.0%	16.05	19.60	17.58
Amerigas Partners LP	3.68	4.0%	44.02	67.38	56.34
Omega Healthcare Inv	2.20	8.0%	36.20	53.59	41.03

Income-oriented securities such as REITs and MLPs tend to score very well under this model, perhaps because capital gains is a secondary consideration for most investors in these two asset classes.

Professional Security Analysis

Perhaps the easiest, non-numeric way to determine stock value is to look to the research of the Certified Financial Analysts who do this for a living. Every major brokerage or investment firm in this county employs an extensive team of financial analysts, each one specializing in a particular sector or industry, who develop complex discounted cash flow models that produce value estimates for hundreds of stocks.

Here are the sources that I think are most professional:

- MORNINGSTAR.COM (free/fee)

  I have already mentioned this website as my favorite source for both financial data and analysis.

  Every aspect of investment portfolio construction is covered in detail, including introductory investment tutorials, economic trends, full data spread sheets, selection screens, diversification, retirement considerations, tax planning, and of course in-depth individual stock analysis (the last requires premium membership – and is well worth it!)

The research here is top rate: very thorough and professional. If you follow the site on a regular basis, you will get to know the commentators and analysts through video presentations on a very personal basis. These interviews – informative, animated, and well paced – are what really set Morningstar apart from other sites.

For premium membership, Morningstar publishes a specific "fair value" estimate, based on the latest model results and updated at least quarterly. However, the site also has a general rating system for stock value in which a number of stars (from one to five) will appear next to the company name. These stars do *not* represent the quality or performance of the stock; instead they represent how the current price relates to the fair value estimate. One star indicates that the current price is substantially over the fair value; hence the stock is quite overvalued. Five stars indicate the exact opposite: The current price is far below the fair value estimate; hence the stock is a real bargain! As you might expect, three stars indicate a stock that is fairly valued. This star ranking is part of the free service, so even without the premium service you will still have a general idea as to stock value.

- **VALUENTUM.COM (fee)**

  Valuentum (a fee site) publishes a specific dollar estimate of fair value, but it also publishes a bell curve probability distribution (range) of fair value with the dollar estimate at the top of the curve. This probably makes good sense, because there are so many assumptions that go into a value estimate that I think a range of probable value is perhaps a better way to approach this whole question.

As mentioned above, Valuentum is in my opinion quite conservative, very anti-debt, and strict in their belief that all dividends must be covered comfortably by free cash flow (see Attachment H). Nevertheless these reports are thorough and the analysis process seems sound and rigorous.

- **FASTGRAPHS.COM (fee)**

This is an interesting site that presents an immediate, clear graphic depiction of a stock's *historic* values (based on operating earnings) plotted against its *historic* market prices. Here you see graphically not just the current price/value positions, but also how price and value have moved against each other over the years. The presentation is dramatically simple: Whenever the black line (price) falls within the green area (earnings), the stock has been undervalued. Whenever the black line lies above the green area, the stock has been expensive. The model also tracks dividends, if they are paid, showing both dividend growth and payout ratio.

Price/value fluctuation over the years is a very helpful way of grasping just how over- or undervalued the stock may be today, compared to the historical examples presented. This is the only site I know that takes an historic approach to value. This site is quite popular with the financial contributors to Seeking Alpha.

- **PARSIMONYRESEARCH.COM (fee)**

Parsimony Research has developed a quantitative stock selection model very similar in concept to the model that I have presented in this book. The main difference is that instead of looking at ten metrics (as our model does), Parsimony considers nearly 50! These are all weighted and blended to produce a single rating number from 1 to 100. Parsimony publishes a range of fair value estimates, which establish a "buy zone." The company alerts its clients whenever a stock enters this zone.

When to Buy: Summary

We have reviewed several methods to determine the current fair/intrinsic value of a security. The earlier methods presented are attractive because they are simple to understand and calculate. As you begin to analyze stocks for potential purchase I would certainly encourage you to become familiar with the P/E, PEG, and Dividend Discount models. In my opinion these are "beginner" approaches that do give you some basic feel for value, both relative to a stock's own past performance as well as to other stocks. However, they are limited in several critical respects, as I have discussed.

I tend to rely much more heavily on the non-perpetual discount model, which actually reflects – at least to some extent – buying and selling stocks in a "real world" context. The tables I have presented for a 15-year holding period were developed using the Net Present Value (NPV) metric which is offered in an Excel spreadsheet. You might wish to develop your own table, using either Excel or some other calculator, to reflect a different holding period, a different discount rate, or a different final capital gain.

Again, I have assumed modest capital gains, so that a non-perpetual fair value calculation which is below the current price is likely to represent an attractive buying opportunity.

I also place a stronger degree of confidence in the fair value estimates published by Morningstar, for the reasons I have discussed. The estimates of Valuentum, Fast Graphs, and Parsimony Research (among others) are also helpful, particularly if they tend to confirm the Morningstar estimate. However, *these last three are formula-driven estimates,* and though the protocols involved appear to be extensive and rigorous, they don't seem to offer the level of individual thought and analysis found on Morningstar.

Discipline: Waiting for Your Price

As you work to determine a fair value for the stocks that rank highest in your final selection screen, you will probably find that some – if not most – of these stocks are currently priced above your calculation of fair value. So you will decide that the time is not right for a purchase. This may be a tough call – particularly for a stock that really excites you! – *but the discipline of restraint is extremely important to develop and apply on a consistent basis*. Keep in mind that waiting for a break or correction in price – even if it only increases your yield by a modest amount at purchase – can have a very pronounced effect on your total return over time as compound interest does its work.

Consider a stock that you could buy today with a yield of 4.0%. Your calculation of fair value shows that the stock is overpriced. You decide to wait until the price drops 10%, at which point the yield will increase to 4.44%. If you believe that the dividend will grow 7% over the next 15 years, at the end of that period your yield would be 11.04% if you bought with a 4.0% yield, compared to 12.26% if you had waited to buy the stock with a 4.44% yield. So a yield difference of just 0.44% at purchase becomes a difference of 1.22% after compound interest takes effect.

Dollar Cost Averaging

Another approach to opening a position in a stock is to buy in gradually over time rather than committing the full amount all at once. A good strategy here is called *Dollar Cost Averaging*. This strategy involves *investing a fixed amount of money with each purchase, rather than buying a fixed number of shares*. By spending a fixed amount each time you buy, you are automatically buying fewer shares when the price is high and more shares when the price is low. Therefore your average cost per share must be lower than if you bought a fixed number of shares with each trade.

When to Sell

For mature investors who do consider the "when" – the timing – of their stock transactions, I think most would invest a fair amount of time trying to determine when to buy, but perhaps less time thinking about when to sell. Yet *the timing of both buy and sell orders is fundamental to one's total return.*

My general observation is that *investors tend to be more logical on the buy side, but more emotional on the sell side.* Before you buy a stock, you have time to think and deliberate. You are – hopefully – calm and rational as you weigh the pros and cons. But after purchase, you develop an emotional attachment to the security in question. This is just natural – you have made a commitment and you want your judgment to be confirmed – both for financial gain as well as for personal pride and ego gratification. To put it simply, *once you're in, you worry – particularly if your primary focus is on capital gains.*

And with that worry – that emotion – comes the very distinct possibility of irrational behavior. If your stock has done well, you may feel the need to *sell now*, and lock in that profit before the market moves against you. If the stock declines, you may feel the need to *sell now*, to avoid any further loss. In either case, *your emotions may lead you to act now – trade now* – which decision may be short-sighted and costly, both in terms of higher transaction fees, lost dividends, and lost appreciation potential.

If I had to pick the most basic mistake that investors make, it would be *panic selling*. The market falls, and the gains which you have in a particular stock are evaporating. Or worse, you don't have any gains at all and your losses are mounting. *If your focus is on capital gains*, you become nervous, apprehensive, and uncomfortable. And so you sell to end the discomfort. In doing so, *you lock in a smaller profit or a larger loss than you had before the market moved against you. You will never be able to recover –* either to a higher gain or a smaller loss – since you have given up on that stock. *Game over!*

Here again we see the advantage of adopting the Dividend Growth Investor philosophy. *Your primary focus is not capital gains, but rather a sustainable, growing stream of income.* You realize that you cannot control the market and you *stop worrying about it.* Well, maybe it still bothers you when the market tanks – that is just human nature and it sure bothers me! – but DGI enables you to *keep your eyes on the prize* – long term income, not short term gain. And as we have discussed, a market correction will provide some attractive buying opportunities. So the DGI approach leads an investor to feel neutral – or perhaps even positive – about a market correction.

So the fundamental DGI approach would essentially fall into the "buy and hold" school of investing. You have researched and screened a security and you feel very positive about the potential for long term income growth. You have determined a fair value that is below market and provides you with some "margin for error." You buy the stock with the full intention of holding it for an indefinite period of time. What then are the conditions under which it would be appropriate to sell?

Dividend Cut

Obviously the biggest shock to a Dividend Growth Investor is to experience a dividend cut. There are many members of the DGI community who would automatically sell any security that cut its dividend. I can certainly sympathize with this feeling, but I don't fully agree with it and I think that each case should be decided based on the particular circumstances of that event.

- **How big a loss will I take if I sell immediately?**

  If the loss is modest, I would sell immediately and accept the loss. If it is large, I would review the company from scratch to try and determine if some price recovery might be possible after the "dividend shock" wore off. If management can make a convincing case that recovery is expected and realistic in the short term – and independent stock analysts agree – I might be tempted to hang on and avoid locking in a larger loss.

- **Is the yield after the cut still attractive?**

  I have related my own story about Century Link, which cut its dividend shortly after my purchase. My yield was over 7% at the time of purchase, and was still well above 5% after the cut. I crunched the numbers again and felt that any further cut was highly unlikely (no further cut has occurred to date), so I stuck with the stock – and its still-attractive dividend – until the price nearly recovered. I then sold because I saw no realistic possibility of near term dividend growth.

- **What are my alternative investment options?**

  If I have no immediate investment option that would provide a satisfactory combination of screen score, yield, and diversification, I might stand pat until such an opportunity arose. I would be careful to avoid moving into a marginal investment simply because I sought to unload an unwanted holding. An alternative here would be to sell and simply hold the cash pending further developments.

- **Has management given any clear warning about a dividend cut?**

  While it is rare, management will on occasion inform its shareholders that a dividend cut may be under consideration. This takes no small amount of transparency and candor, as well as self-confidence in the long term strength of the firm and in the sophistication of its shareholders. If the reasons for a possible cut are stated clearly and a near-term, credible recovery strategy is well presented, I would be inclined to stay with management of this caliber.

- **What about a dividend freeze?**

  I think that a dividend freeze is essentially the same thing as a dividend cut. The company is telling you that it is experiencing cash flow issues, and while it has avoided the outright stigma of a cut, *it has stopped growing its dividend.* I might give the company just a little more slack, but not much. A dividend freeze is often a prelude to a dividend cut, and I would look very carefully at the payout ratio to see how far it has deteriorated. If the deterioration is significant, I would treat the freeze just as I would treat a cut and go through the steps listed immediately above.

Deterioration In Fundamentals

Sooner or later, *every* company is going to encounter an earnings slump. It is simply in the nature of economic and commercial activity that profit contraction will happen sooner or later, and that is why I usually don't worry too much about quarterly earnings announcements. Unless such announcements are quite severe and startling, I am not going to spend much time reviewing them. Day traders might pay attention, but long term DGI investors have better things to do!

But what if the company begins to experience a more prolonged downward trend? This brings us back to our discussion of "Qualitative Considerations" in Section Three. There are always long-term trends at work which gradually undermine certain companies while boosting others. These trends develop from social, technological, geopolitical, and economic forces which constantly change the global, national, and local dynamics of supply and demand. New products and services arise, grow, mature, and eventually diminish, perhaps even disappear.

So if earnings remain depressed for more than a few quarters, the challenge for the DGI investor is to determine what changes have taken place, and are these changes fundamental rather than cyclical or temporary? The basic question should be: Have we *seen this before? Has the company experienced this problem in the past? If so, how was it resolved and how long did it take?*

This can be a very tough call. Management will obviously put a positive spin on recovery plans, but how long should you wait to see clear improvement? There is no simple answer to that, as it depends on your own level of patience and your assessment of the situation. But pay special attention to:

- Changes in consumer tastes, preferences, and behavior
- Dated products and technology
- Loss of competitive position
- Loss of economic moat
- Loss of market share
- Prolonged stagnation or decline in sales and/or operating income
- Significant increase in the dividend payout ratio
- Significant increase in debt levels
- Customer/Supplier concentration

These are in fact the same questions you explored when you first bought the stock, so the time has come to revisit these same issues. If you still feel comfortable, you may elect to hold on. If not, then move on. But this will not be a panic sell; it will be a considered, rational exit. You may still lose money, but not because of fear. And you will have learned something in the process that will help you grow as an experienced and more mature investor.

Taking a Profit

You have achieved a considerable unrealized profit in a particular stock. How do you determine when or if you should sell the stock, realize your profit, and reinvest the proceeds?

The first step would be to go through the mechanics of updating the current fair value of the stock, as we have outlined at the beginning of this chapter. If this review leads you to believe that the stock is significantly overvalued, then the timing may be right for a sale.

A second consideration would be to look at the current dividend yield. As the price has gone up, the dividend yield has probably gone down. As a basic rule of thumb, if the current market yield is now below the minimum yield you would require on a new purchase, this would be a strong incentive to sell the stock and reinvest the proceeds in a stock with a higher yield.

An example would help here. Assume that you purchased Company A for $50.00/share, with a dividend of $1.50 and therefore a yield at purchase of 3.0%. The stock price increases to $70.00, a gain of 40%. If the dividend has not increased, the new market yield is $1.50/$70.00, or 2.14%. Since you would not *buy* a stock with a market yield that low, you should not *keep* a stock with a market yield that low. You can sell the stock and reinvest the proceeds in any stock – with a yield above 2.14% – and increase your dividend income, as follows:

Sell stock for $70.00. You are giving up a dividend of $1.50.

If your minimum opening yield is 3.0%, then the $70.00 reinvestment will yield a dividend of $2.10

You have increased your income by 40% with the same yield at purchase as your original investment.

I think there is an important insight here. *Your purpose in selling is not to "make a profit," the goal of a capital gains investor. Rather, it is to increase your income stream. In other words,* buying low and selling high is not an end in itself. Rather, it is a step which enables you to achieve your true goal – a higher level of sustained cash flow.

Rebalancing

On an annual basis, I think it is important to review the diversification of your portfolio. You may find that you have a higher concentration in one sector, industry, or asset class than you originally intended. This concentration may be the result of price appreciation or depreciation in certain sectors, or because of purchases and sales made during the year. In any event, you may wish to sell certain stocks to reduce concentration and/or buy certain stocks in increase concentration, thereby re-establishing the diversification profile that you desire.

You Need The Cash

Unless your portfolio is 100% organic – your ultimate goal – then you will periodically have to sell securities to pay your bills. What you sell will depend on a number of possible factors. First, it will depend on your age – if you are in retirement and need cash now, you will probably look first to sell stocks with lower yields. If you are younger, then dividend growth becomes the most important factor. Or you might decide to sell those stocks with the lowest updated screen scores. Or you might consider selling those stocks which will not cause an imbalance in your diversification. Another thought would be to look at your year-to-date capital gains (or losses) and select a stock to sell based on income tax considerations. But the main point is to give your decision a good amount of thought and take care not to make a random and hasty decision.

Periodic Portfolio Review

I review every security in my portfolio twice a year. Since most companies have a December fiscal date, these reviews occur primarily in late February and late August when the year-end and mid-year financial reports are published. These are actually good times for me to perform the reviews since they do not normally interfere with holidays or vacations. Morningstar will update its spreadsheets within a day or two after the reports are published, so in most cases you will not have to review the actual reports themselves to update the screen scores. However, REIT and MLP updates will require review of the actual reports to determine FFO and DCF.

I perform a complete update of the qualitative and quantitative aspects of the company, just as if I were reviewing the company for initial purchase. In addition to any significant qualitative change in fundamentals, I pay attention to quantitative metrics that are likely to change more quickly, including:

- Percentage change in most recent dividend/distribution
- Change in dividend payout ratio
- Change in CFO growth
- Weighted average total return

I calculate a new final screen score and compare it to the preceding score. If there are any significant changes, I write a brief summary on the top of the form as to what has happened and why. I also note significant qualitative/fundamental developments, if any.

It is probable that a few of your holdings will show a significant deterioration in qualitative and/or quantitative strength. On the quantitative side, I am usually OK to hold a stock with any score above 650, but would find it very hard to continue holding a security if the score fell below 600. For scores between 600-650, I generally put the stock on my "watch" list and follow it more closely. I may set a target price for a watch list stock and sell if that price is achieved.

On the qualitative side, a clear deterioration in fundamentals might lead you to sell, as discussed above.

This semiannual exercise will help to insure that your portfolio remains strong, and that any deterioration is discovered and analyzed in a timely fashion so that prompt action may be taken before the problem gets too far advanced for recovery. Note that this exercise is also a good time to check the diversification of your portfolio and rebalance if necessary.

Summary: Section Five

When you buy a new car, what do you do? As an educated consumer, you would price out comparable models, determine a fair value for your trade in, and head for the dealer with a firm price in mind.

Hopefully you can negotiate an acceptable price. But if you can't, you walk away from the deal.

That last sentence is the key – whether you are buying a car or buying a security. First you develop some pretty firm idea as to what price range you are willing to accept, and if you ultimately can't find that price – *then you don't buy*. This takes will power, especially when a stock produces a very strong screen score in an asset class or industry sector that really excites you. But if you have the discipline to wait for your price, you take a giant step to achieving the long term goal of a 100% organic portfolio.

This chapter has reviewed several methods which will help you determine the price you are willing to pay for a security. Some of these methods are easy to understand and calculate, but are based on assumptions that are – in my opinion – unrealistic and are therefore of limited value. I prefer discounted cash flow models that attempt to reflect how investments may behave over time in real world circumstances. If you are comfortable with the assumptions I have made, you can use the discounted non-perpetual tables listed in this section to determine fair value, or you can derive your own table using the Net Present Value metric of Excel or some other calculator. You can also consider the fair value estimates published by Morningstar and other on-line investment services.

Several final thoughts occur to me on this subject:

First, make sure you follow the sequence of stock selection and investment as it is presented in this book; that is, the *first step is to determine quality, the second step is to determine fair value.* Don't look to determine a fair price before you have analyzed what you're buying! Make sure that you don't get attracted to a stock just because it has a high yield and looks undervalued. There may be a good reason for that high yield – low quality! As Warren Buffett says:

> **"It is better to pay a fair price for a good stock**
> **Than a good price for a fair stock."**

Second, the estimation of a fair value is not a "one and done" event. This exercise should be repeated at least once or twice a year. If you review the screen score of your portfolio twice a year, then I would update my fair value estimate at that time as well. You will also want to update the value estimates for stocks on your watch list – stocks that you want to buy when the price is right. By updating these value estimates, buying and/or selling opportunities may appear.

Third, understand that no matter how accurate you think your value estimate may be, the market may totally disagree with you, and it may take months to see your price and the market price converge, if in fact they converge at all. Frustrating yes, but hang tough and stick to your guns!

Finally, don't forget the importance of timing on the sell side. Remember that buying at the right price *determines* the ultimate total return, while selling at the right price *achieves* this return.

Conclusion

Well, there you have it.

That's my case for Dividend Growth Investing.

It has been a pleasure for me to write this book and I hope that it has been a pleasure for you to read it. More importantly, I hope it has motivated you to take a hard look at the way you think about investing and the way you now go about it.

Investors like me who are approaching or entering retirement began investing at an incredibly fortunate moment in time. The stock market went on a 17-year tear at the end of the twentieth century, doubling our money every four and one half years. That is what we experienced, and that is what we came to expect. Dividends and interest meant virtually nothing to us. *Capital gains were a given.*

Then we moved forward and looked at stock market performance over the last twenty years. We saw that during this period, the market rewarded (1995-1999), then crushed (2000-2002), then rewarded (2003-2007), then *really* crushed (2008), and then rewarded (2009-2015) investors. We saw how investors who did everything right in amassing a sizeable portfolio for retirement fell far short of achieving sustained income, just by the random chance of unlucky market timing. Some were in fact completely wiped out within a dozen years. And this is not ancient history. *This just happened!* We all remember this. We all lived through this.

I am not going to make any predictions about the future of the stock market. I will let the facts – recent facts – speak for themselves. *If you rely on capital gains to fund your retirement, then you are not in control of your financial future. You may have done everything right, yet through no fault of your own, you may fall far short of achieving financial independence.*

Dividend Growth Investing is an approach to solving this dilemma. It may not work for everybody because it requires time, discipline, focus, and a reasonably steady stream of income that permits consistent savings over the years. But for those who possess these qualifications, it is an approach that offers you:

- **Control** over your investments, instead of your investments controlling you;

- **Consistent**, increasing returns over time;

- The **Comfort** of a Sleep Well At Night (SWAN) portfolio!

Best Wishes!
Good Luck!
Steve Bennett
November 2015

Getting Started

Well now that we have you totally jazzed to start investing, there are a number of things that you will have to do to get started. I think you will be pleasantly surprised at how easy – and inexpensive – the entire process is.

Setting up a Brokerage Account:
When I started investing over 30 years ago, discount brokerage was still in its infancy, led by Charles Schwab in 1975. And of course there was no internet and no online anything! So I would walk uptown and sit down with my broker and have a pleasant chat and maybe ask him to buy something for me.

He made a straight commission of about $35 a trade, or something like that. So I didn't trade much and he didn't make much money from my account. But he was a nice guy and somehow he managed to make enough money off of *somebody* to retire.

Well those days are long gone. There are now a host of online discount brokers to choose from, offering a variety of sophisticated research and training tools, stock selection screens, and instant trading platforms. Fees per trade range from just over $4.00 to $10.00 and in general that is all you should have to pay. Remember that you are now making your own investment decisions, so if you have been using an investment advisor, you will never have to pay that fee again. So right off the top *you are saving at least one full percent – or more – of your portfolio balance every year by managing your own money.* You're off to a good start!

My brokerage account is with Scottrade. They charge a flat fee of $7.00 per trade, and that's it. There are no minimum or maintenance fees beyond that. What I really like is that Scottrade has over 500 office locations throughout the country, by far the largest retail branch network of any discount broker. I do all my trading online, but I do enjoy the comfort of actually sitting down with a registered rep to conduct business and discuss questions – just like the old days! But that convenience will mean little to younger investors who are more comfortable with online transactions and money transfers than I am.

So just Google "discount brokers" and you will get a quick list of several other firms that have far fewer offices – or none at all – but may offer lower trading costs. There are reviews you can read as well. I really don't think you can go wrong with any of the national brokerage organizations that have been around for 20 years or longer.

Account Maintenance:

I maintain a one page, two-sided write up (evaluation form) on every security I purchase. The front side contains a brief description of the company and all the metric values I need to calculate the preliminary and the final screen scores (see sample form on page 134). The back side contains the scoring matrix (see page 152). I maintain these as physical pages in a three-ring binder, which for an old guy like me is easier to access than a computer file.

As indicated above, I review every security twice a year. I update all the metrics after the annual and semiannual reports are published, and rescore the security. Depending on the result, I may take action, as outlined at the end of the last section.

Perhaps the nicest part of the review process is entering in a new, higher dividend amount. This shows me that my primary objective is being met. And make sure to keep track of special dividends! To be conservative I do not count on them as part of my current or projected yield, but they certainly put a smile on my face and solidify my conviction that management is shareholder friendly!

I keep track of my securities by dividing them into the following categories:

Equities (C Corporations)

Equity Funds (CEFs invested in equities)

High Yield (High Yield Bond CEFs and Business Development CEFs)

REITs

MLPs

Municipal Bonds (CEFs)

Every quarter I update my "Security Inventory" report, which is structured as follows (see next page).

At the bottom of the page I add on all other sources of income, including social security, pensions, and annuities. This gives me a running total throughout the year of total expected income. The five year projections show me how my income is expected to grow and what level of protection I should achieve against inflation.

Calculators:
Excel spreadsheet
As I mentioned at the beginning of this book, I would be happy to share my Excel spreadsheet with anyone who would like have it. You can request it by sending an Email to: shustonbennett@gmail.com.

Business calculator
I calculate weighted average growth rates (WAGR) with an Excel spreadsheet, but use a business calculator to calculate compound average growth rates (CAGR). We use CAGR to calculate future dividend yield and share buyback yield, so you will need to have a business calculator for this purpose.

Securities	Shares	Annual Dividend	Annual Income	Cost	Yield @ Cost	Projected Div Growth	5 yr Proj Yield	5 yr Proj Income
Equities (List all individual stocks)								
Equity Funds (List all individual funds)								
High Yield (List all individual CEFs or BDCs)								
REITs (List all individual REITs)								
MLPs (List all individual MLPs)								
Municipal Bonds (List all individual Bond CEFs)								

ATTACHMENTS

Attachment **A**

40-Year Savings Scenario

Attachment A represents a hypothetical example of savings for retirement over a 40-year period.

An individual with a salary of $40,000 at age 25 receives salary raises of 3% every year. He begins saving and saves $2,000 per year over years 25-29. Beginning at age 30, his savings increase to $3,000 per year. At each 5-year anniversary thereafter, his savings increase by $1,000 per year.

His 40-year salary and savings pattern looks like this:

	Annual Savings	5 Year Savings	Start Salary	End Salary	Savings/ Start Salary
Ages 25-29:	$2,000	$10,000	$40,000	$46,370	5.00% per year
Ages 30-34:	$3,000	$15,000	$46,370	$53,756	6.47%
Ages 35-39:	$4,000	$20,000	$53,756	$62,318	7.44%
Ages 40-44:	$5,000	$25,000	$62,318	$72,244	8.02%
Ages 45-49:	$6,000	$30,000	$72,244	$83,751	8.31%
Ages 50-54:	$7,000	$35,000	$83,751	$97,090	8.36%
Ages 55-59:	$8,000	$40,000	$97,090	$112,554	8.24%
Ages 60-64:	$9,000	$45,000	$112,554	$130,481	8.00%
		$220,000			

This is of course a hypothetical example. However, I feel that a salary of $40,000 at age 25 is a fairly reasonable assumption and that annual raises of 3% seem quite modest and would barely cover inflation in most years. The five-year savings bump ups may be somewhat aggressive, but at no time do annual savings exceed 8.4% of annual income, which I think a disciplined saver could accommodate. Note also that the savings rate gradually increases from 5.00% up to 8.36%, allowing for less savings/more expenditure in the early years.

The total amount invested over 40 years is $220,000. The attachment assumes that all savings can be invested at an ongoing rate of 6.5%. If one assumes a *constant* dividend yield of 6.5% with dividend reinvestment, then *with no capital gains whatsoever over a 40-year period*, the total portfolio would grow to $748,416 by retirement age.

I think the assumptions of a *constant (no growth) dividend yield and no capital gains* are extremely conservative and in fact run counter to the results that this book tries to demonstrate. So on balance I think that a final portfolio value of nearly $750,000 is very realistic and attainable.

So here is another example of the power of dividend reinvestment. With a total investment of $220,000, we wind up with a portfolio of nearly $750,000. But notice that we are *only using half of the compounding power we discussed in Section I. We are not increasing the dividend yield*. We are assuming no dividend increases. Clearly our investor would not pick stocks that did not grow their dividends. So there is no doubt that with even modest dividend growth, our portfolio would be substantially higher.

The point of this exercise is to show again that portfolio development may be concentrated into a brief period of time. In this example, the halfway point of value creation ($374,208) occurs shortly after age 55, when the portfolio totals $334,218. It can be calculated that this point occurs at age 56.2 years, or 31.2 years into the 40-year period. *This means that the second half of value creation occurs in just 8.8 years, or just 22% of the full investment period.*

And so think again about what would have happened to this portfolio if:

- The investor did not seek income and invested for capital gains;
- This 8.8 year period started at the end of the last century.

ATTACHMENT A

Age Range:	25-29	30-34	35-39	40-44	45-49	50-54	55-59	60-64
Total Age Range Savings:	10,000	15,000	20,000	25,000	30,000	35,000	40,000	45,000
Dividend Yield:	6.50%	6.50%	6.50%	6.50%	6.50%	6.50%	6.50%	6.50%

VALUE AT AGE

Contributions:	30	35	40	45	50	55	60	65
Age 25	2,740	3,754	5,143	7,047	9,655	13,228	18,124	24,832
Age 26	2,573	3,525	4,829	6,617	9,066	12,421	17,018	23,316
Age 27	2,415	3,309	4,534	6,213	8,512	11,663	15,979	21,893
Age 28	2,268	3,107	4,258	5,834	7,993	10,951	15,004	20,557
Age 29	2,130	2,918	3,998	5,478	7,505	10,282	14,088	19,302
Total Value by Age 30	**12,126**							
Age 30		4,110	5,631	7,715	10,570	14,483	19,843	27,186
Age 31		3,859	5,287	7,244	9,925	13,599	18,632	25,527
Age 32		3,623	4,964	6,802	9,319	12,769	17,494	23,969
Age 33		3,402	4,661	6,387	8,751	11,989	16,427	22,506
Age 34		3,195	4,377	5,997	8,217	11,258	15,424	21,132
Total Value by Age 35		**34,802**						
Age 35			5,480	7,508	10,287	14,094	19,310	26,457
Age 36			5,145	7,050	9,659	13,234	18,132	24,842
Age 37			4,831	6,619	9,069	12,426	17,025	23,326
Age 38			4,536	6,215	8,516	11,668	15,986	21,902
Age 39			4,260	5,836	7,996	10,956	15,010	20,565
Total Value by Age 40			**71,934**					

Attachment A, continued next page

ATTACHMENT A

SAVING FOR RETIREMENT: 40 YEAR INVESTMENT PERIOD

Age Range:	25-29	30-34	35-39	40-44	45-49	50-54	55-59	60-64
Total Age Range Savings:	10,000	15,000	20,000	25,000	30,000	35,000	40,000	45,000
Dividend Yield:	**6.50%**	**6.50%**	**6.50%**	**6.50%**	**6.50%**	**6.50%**	**6.50%**	**6.50%**
VALUE AT AGE	30	35	40	45	50	55	60	65
Age 40				6,850	9,385	12,859	17,618	24,138
Age 41				6,432	8,812	12,074	16,542	22,665
Age 42				6,039	8,274	11,337	15,533	21,281
Age 43				5,671	7,769	10,645	14,585	19,983
Age 44				5,325	7,295	9,995	13,695	18,763
Total Value by Age 45				**128,879**				
Age 45					8,220	11,262	15,431	21,141
Age 46					7,718	10,575	14,489	19,851
Age 47					7,247	9,929	13,604	18,639
Age 48					6,805	9,323	12,774	17,502
Age 49					6,390	8,754	11,994	16,434
Total Value by Age 50					**212,955**			
Age 50						9,590	13,139	18,002
Age 51						9,005	12,337	16,904
Age 52						8,455	11,584	15,872
Age 53						7,939	10,877	14,903
Age 54						7,455	10,213	13,994
Total Value by Age 55						**334,218**		

Attachment A, continued next page

ATTACHMENT A

SAVING FOR RETIREMENT: 40 YEAR INVESTMENT PERIOD

	25-29	30-34	35-39	40-44	45-49	50-54	55-59	60-64
Age Range:	25-29	30-34	35-39	40-44	45-49	50-54	55-59	60-64
Total Age Range Savings:	10,000	15,000	20,000	25,000	30,000	35,000	40,000	45,000
Dividend Yield:	**6.50%**	**6.50%**	**6.50%**	**6.50%**	**6.50%**	**6.50%**	**6.50%**	**6.50%**
VALUE AT AGE	30	35	40	45	50	55	60	65
Age 55							10,960	15,017
Age 56							10,291	14,100
Age 57							9,663	13,239
Age 58							9,073	12,431
Age 59							8,520	11,673
Total Value by Age 60							**506,418**	
Age 60								12,330
Age 61								11,578
Age 62								10,871
Age 63								10,208
Age 64								9,585
Total Value by Age 65								**748,416**

FIRST HALF OF VALUE CREATION OCCURS AFTER 31.2 YEARS

SECOND HALF OCCURS IN 8.8 YEARS — 22% OF TOTAL PERIOD

Attachment **B1**
Retirement Scenarios

The tables on the following pages show what would have happened to the portfolios of ten investors, all of whom retire at age 65 in sequential years beginning in 1998. The assumptions for each retiree are:

Portfolio at Retirement:$1,000,000
First Annual Draw:$60,000
Inflation:2.0%

Investment Strategy: All retirees are capital gains investors who do not buy dividend stocks.

The retirees believe that their portfolios will return 6.5% per year in capital appreciation, below the historic nominal growth rate. Given this rate, the investors calculate that their portfolios should last 32 years before exhaustion – to age 97.

The tables may be read as follows:

VALUE +/-: This multiple represents the gain or loss of the S&P 500 average for each year.

For example, in 1998 the S&P increased from 970 to 1229, an increase of 26.7%. Therefore we multiply the starting balance of $1,000,000 by 1.267 to determine the value of the portfolio at the end of 1998.

YE VALUE: The product of the *previous* year end balance (YE BALNC) times *current* year (VALUE +/-)

DRAW: The amount withdrawn from the portfolio every year to cover living expenses. This amount increases by 2.0% each year due to inflation. This amount is deducted from YE VALUE to determine yearend balance (YE BALNC).

YE BALNC: Year End Balance. This is the closing amount of the portfolio for any given year. It represents the year end value (YE VALUE) less the DRAW amount for that year.

Year End Balances for 2014 (or year of exhaustion) are underlined in bold print. Note that three of the retirees have reached the point of portfolio exhaustion by 2014.

ATTACHMENT B1: RETIREMENT SCENARIOS

RETIRE 1/1/1998 1,000,000

	YE VALUE	- DRAW =	YE BALNC	VALUE+/-
1998	1267000	-60,000	1207000	1.2670
1999	1442727	-61,200	1381527	1.1953
2000	1241440	-62,424	1179016	0.8986
2001	1025390	-63,672	961718	0.8697
2002	737253	-64,945	672308	0.7666
2003	849529	-66,244	783285	1.2636
2004	853702	-67,568	786134	1.0899
2005	809482	-68,920	740562	1.0297
2006	841427	-70,298	771129	1.1362
2007	798350	-71,703	726647	1.0353
2008	446960	-73,138	373822	0.6151
2009	461596	-74,600	386996	1.2348
2010	436299	-76,092	360207	1.1274
2011	360207	-77,614	282593	1.0000
2012	360574	-79,167	241407	1.1344
2013	312839	-80,750	232089	1.2959
2014	258686	-82,365	**176321**	1.1146

RETIRE 1/1/1999 1,000,000

	YE VALUE	- DRAW =	YE BALNC	VALUE+/-
1999	1195300	-60,000	1135300	1.1953
2000	1020181	-61,200	958981	0.8986
2001	834025	-62,424	771601	0.8697
2002	591510	-63,672	527838	0.7666
2003	666976	-64,945	602031	1.2636
2004	656153	-66,244	589909	1.0899
2005	607430	-67,568	539862	1.0297
2006	613391	-68,920	544471	1.1362
2007	563690	-70,298	493392	1.0353
2008	303486	-71,703	231783	0.6151
2009	286205	-73,138	213067	1.2348
2010	240212	-74,600	165612	1.1274
2011	165612	-76,092	89520	1.0000
2012	101552	-77,614	23938	1.1344
2013	31021	-79,167	**-48146**	1.2959

Attachment B1, continued next page

ATTACHMENT B1   RETIREMENT SCENARIOS (continued)

RETIRE	**1/1/2000**	1,000,000		
YE	VALUE	- DRAW =	YE BALNC	VALUE+/-
2000	898600	-60,000	838600	0.8986
2001	729330	-61,200	668130	0.8697
2002	512189	-62,424	449765	0.7666
2003	568323	-63,672	504651	1.2636
2004	550019	-64,945	485074	1.0899
2005	499481	-66,244	433237	1.0297
2006	492243	-67,568	424675	1.1362
2007	439666	-68,920	370746	1.0353
2008	228046	-70,298	157748	0.6151
2009	194787	-71,704	123083	1.2348
2010	138764	-73,138	65626	1.1274
2011	65626	-74,601	**-8975**	1.0000

RETIRE	**1/1/2001**	1,000,000		
YE	VALUE	- DRAW =	YE BALNC	VALUE+/-
2001	869700	-60,000	809700	0.8697
2002	620716	-61,200	559516	0.7666
2003	707004	-62,424	644580	1.2636
2004	702528	-63,672	638856	1.0899
2005	657830	-64,945	592885	1.0297
2006	673636	-66,244	607392	1.1362
2007	628833	-67,568	561265	1.0353
2008	345234	-68,920	276314	0.6151
2009	341193	-70,298	270895	1.2348
2010	305407	-71,704	233703	1.1274
2011	233703	-73,138	160565	1.0000
2012	182145	-74,601	107544	1.1344
2013	139366	-76,093	63273	1.2959
2014	70524	-77,615	**-7091**	1.1146

Attachment B1, continued next page

ATTACHMENT B1: RETIREMENT SCENARIOS (continued)

RETIRE	1/1/2002 YE VALUE	-DRAW=	1,000,000 YE BALNC	VALUE+/-
2002	766600	-60,000	706600	0.7666
2003	892860	-61,200	831660	1.2636
2004	906426	-62,424	844002	1.0899
2005	869069	-63,672	805397	1.0297
2006	915092	-64,945	850147	1.1362
2007	880157	-66,244	813913	1.0353
2008	500638	-67,568	433070	0.6151
2009	534755	-68,920	465835	1.2348
2010	525182	-70,298	454884	1.1274
2011	454884	-71,704	383180	1.0000
2012	434679	-73,138	361541	1.1344
2013	468522	-74,601	393921	1.2959
2014	439064	-76,093	**362971**	1.1146

RETIRE	1/1/2003 YE VALUE	-DRAW=	1,000,000 YE BALNC	VALUE+/-
2003	1263600	-60,000	1203600	1.2636
2004	1311804	-61,200	1250604	1.0899
2005	1287747	-62,424	1225323	1.0297
2006	1392212	-63,672	1328540	1.1362
2007	1375437	-64,945	1310492	1.0353
2008	806084	-66,244	739840	0.6151
2009	913554	-67,568	845986	1.2348
2010	953765	-68,920	884845	1.1274
2011	884845	-70,298	814547	1.0000
2012	924022	-71,704	852318	1.1344
2013	1104518	-73,138	1031380	1.2959
2014	1149577	-74,601	**1074976**	1.1146

Attachment B1, continued next page

ATTACHMENT B1: RETIREMENT SCENARIOS (continued)

RETIRE	1/1/2004 YE VALUE	-DRAW=	YE BALNC 1,000,000	VALUE+/-
2004	1089900	-60,000	1029900	1.0899
2005	1060488	-61,200	999288	1.0297
2006	1135391	-62,424	1072967	1.1362
2007	1110843	-63,672	1047171	1.0353
2008	644115	-64,945	579170	0.6151
2009	715159	-66,244	648915	1.2348
2010	731587	-67,568	664019	1.1274
2011	664019	-68,920	595099	1.0000
2012	675080	-70,298	604782	1.1344
2013	783737	-71,704	712033	1.2959
2014	793632	-73,138	**720494**	1.1146

RETIRE	1/1/2005 YE VALUE	-DRAW=	YE BALNC 1,000,000	VALUE+/-
2005	1029700	-60,000	969700	1.0297
2006	1101773	-61,200	1040573	1.1362
2007	1077305	-62,424	1014881	1.0353
2008	624254	-63,672	560582	0.6151
2009	692206	-64,945	627261	1.2348
2010	707174	-66,244	640930	1.1274
2011	640930	-67,568	573362	1.0000
2012	650422	-68,920	581502	1.1344
2013	753568	-70,298	683270	1.2959
2014	761573	-71,704	**689869**	1.1146

Attachment B1, continued next page

ATTACHMENT B1: RETIREMENT SCENARIOS (continued)

RETIRE	1/1/2006		1,000,000	
2006	1136200	-60,000	1076200	1.1362
2007	1114190	-61,200	1052990	1.0353
2008	647694	-62,424	585270	0.6151
2009	722691	-63,672	659019	1.2348
2010	742979	-64,945	678034	1.1274
2011	678034	-66,244	611790	1.0000
2012	694014	-67,568	626446	1.1344
2013	811811	-68,920	742891	1.2959
2014	828027	-70,298	**757729**	1.1146

RETIRE	1/1/2007		1,000,000	
2007	1035300	-60,000	975300	1.0353
2008	599907	-61,200	538707	0.6151
2009	665195	-62,424	602771	1.2348
2010	679565	-63,672	615893	1.1274
2011	615893	-64,945	550948	1.0000
2012	624995	-66,244	558751	1.1344
2013	724085	-67,568	656517	1.2959
2014	731754	-68,920	**662834**	1.1146

Attachment B2

The assumptions here are the same as Attachment B1 *except that our investors are now buying dividend paying securities.*

This means that we are using the S&P Total Return Index to determine portfolio performance.

ATTACHMENT B2: RETIREMENT SCENARIOS

RETIRE 1/1/1998	YE VAL	DRAW	YE BAL	VALUE+/-
			1000000	
1998	1286000	-60,000	1226000	1.286
1999	1483460	-61,200	1422260	1.210
2000	1292834	-62,424	1,230,410	0.909
2001	1083991	-63,672	1020319	0.881
2002	794829	-64,945	729883	0.779
2003	939360	-66,244	873116	1.287
2004	967413	-67,568	899845	1.108
2005	943937	-68,920	875017	1.049
2006	1013270	-70,298	942972	1.158
2007	994835	-71,703	923132	1.055
2008	581573	-73,138	508435	0.630
2009	642662	-74,600	568062	1.264
2010	653839	-76,092	577747	1.151
2011	589880	-77,614	512266	1.021
2012	594228	-79,167	515061	1.160
2013	681941	-80,750	601191	1.324
2014	683355	-82,365	**601189**	1.137

RETIRE 1/1/1999	YE VAL	DRAW	YE BAL	VALUE+/-
			1000000	
1999	1210000	-60,000	1150000	1.210
2000	1045350	-61,200	984150	0.909
2001	867036	-62,424	804612	0.881
2002	626792	-63,672	563120	0.779
2003	724736	-64,945	659791	1.287
2004	731049	-66,244	664805	1.108
2005	697380	-67,568	629812	1.049
2006	729322	-68,920	660402	1.158
2007	696724	-70,298	626426	1.055
2008	394648	-71,703	322945	0.630
2009	408203	-73,138	335065	1.264
2010	385659	-74,600	311059	1.151
2011	317592	-76,092	241499	1.021
2012	280139	-77,614	202525	1.160
2013	268143	-79,167	188976	1.324
2014		-80,750	**134115**	1.137

Attachment B2, continued next page

ATTACHMENT B2: RETIREMENT SCENARIOS (continued)

RETIRE	**1/1/2000**		1000000	
	YE VALUE	DRAW	YE BALNC	VALUE+/-
2000	909000	-60,000	849000	0.909
2001	747969	-61,200	686769	0.881
2002	534993	-62,424	472569	0.779
2003	608196	-63,672	544524	1.287
2004	603332	-64,945	538387	1.108
2005	564769	-66,244	498525	1.049
2006	577291	-67,568	509723	1.158
2007	537758	-68,920	468838	1.055
2008	295368	-70,298	225070	0.630
2009	284488	-71,703	212785	1.264
2010	244916	-73,138	171778	1.151
2011	175384	-74,600	100784	1.021
2012	116910	-76,092	40818	1.160
2013	54043	-77,614	**-23570**	1.324

RETIRE	**1/1/2001**		1000000	
	YE VALUE	DRAW	YE BALNC	VALUE+/-
2001	881000	-60,000	821000	0.881
2002	639559	-61,200	578359	0.779
2003	744348	-62,424	681924	1.287
2004	755571	-63,672	691899	1.108
2005	725802	-64,945	660857	1.049
2006	765272	-66,244	699028	1.158
2007	737474	-67,568	669906	1.055
2008	422041	-68,920	353121	0.630
2009	446345	-70,298	376047	1.264
2010	432830	-71,703	361127	1.151
2011	368711	-73,138	295573	1.021
2012	342864	-74,600	268264	1.160
2013	355182	-76,092	279090	1.324
2014	317326	-77,614	**239712**	1.137

Attachment B2, continued next page

ATTACHMENT B2
S&P TOTAL RETURN

RETIRE 1/1/2002	YE VAL	DRAW	YE BAL	VALUE+/-
			1000000	
2002	779000	-60,000	719000	0.779
2003	925353	-61,200	864153	1.287
2004	957481	-62,424	895057	1.108
2005	938915	-63,672	875243	1.049
2006	1013531	-64,945	948586	1.158
2007	1000758	-66,244	934514	1.055
2008	588744	-67,568	521176	0.630
2009	658766	-68,920	589846	1.264
2010	678913	-70,298	608615	1.151
2011	621396	-71,703	549693	1.021
2012	637644	-73,138	564506	1.160
2013	747406	-74,600	672806	1.324
2014	764981	-76,092	**688889**	1.137

RETIRE 1/1/2003	YE VAL	DRAW	YE BAL	VALUE+/-
			1000000	
2003	1287000	-60,000	1227000	1.287
2004	1359516	-61,200	1298316	1.108
2005	1361933	-62,424	1299509	1.049
2006	1504831	-63,672	1441159	1.158
2007	1520423	-64,945	1455478	1.055
2008	916951	-66,244	850707	0.630
2009	1075294	-67,568	1007726	1.264
2010	1159892	-68,920	1090972	1.151
2011	1113883	-70,298	1043585	1.021
2012	1210558	-71,703	1138855	1.160
2013	1507845	-73,138	1434707	1.324
2014	1631261	-74,600	**1556661**	1.137

Attachment B2, continued next page

ATTACHMENT B2: S&P TOTAL RETURN

RETIRE	**1/1/2004**		1,000,000	
	YE VAL	DRAW	YE BAL	VALUE+/-
2004	1108000	-60,000	1048000	1.108
2005	1099352	-61,200	1038152	1.049
2006	1202180	-62,424	1139756	1.158
2007	1202442	-63,672	1138770	1.055
2008	717425	-64,945	652480	0.630
2009	824734	-66,244	758491	1.264
2010	873023	-67,568	805454	1.151
2011	822369	-68,920	753449	1.021
2012	874001	-70,298	803703	1.160
2013	1064103	-71,703	992400	1.324
2014	1128359	-73,138	**1055221**	1.137

RETIRE	**1/1/2005**		1,000,000	
	YE VAL	DRAW	YE BAL	VALUE+/-
2005	1049000	-60,000	989000	1.049
2006	1145262	-61,200	1084062	1.158
2007	1143685	-62,424	1081261	1.055
2008	681194	-63,672	617522	0.630
2009	780548	-64,945	715603	1.264
2010	823659	-66,244	757415	1.151
2011	773321	-67,568	705753	1.021
2012	818674	-68,920	749754	1.160
2013	992674	-70,298	922376	1.324
2014	1048741	-71,703	**977038**	1.137

Attachment B2, continued next page

ATTACHMENT B2
S&P TOTAL RETURN (continued)

RETIRE	1/1/2006		1000000	
	YE VAL	DRAW	YE BAL	VALUE+/-
2006	1158000	-60,000	1098000	1.158
2007	1158390	-61,200	1097190	1.055
2008	691229	-62,424	628805	0.630
2009	794810	-63,672	731138	1.264
2010	841540	-64,945	776595	1.151
2011	792903	-66,244	726659	1.021
2012	842925	-67,568	775357	1.160
2013	1026573	-68,920	957653	1.324
2014	1088851	-70,298	**1018553**	1.137

RETIRE	1/1/2007		1000000	
	YE VAL	DRAW	YE BAL	VALUE+/-
2007	1055000	-60,000	995000	1.055
2008	626850	-61,200	565650	0.630
2009	714981	-62,424	652557	1.264
2010	751093	-63,672	687421	1.151
2011	701857	-64,945	636912	1.021
2012	738818	-66,244	672574	1.160
2013	890488	-67,568	822920	1.324
2014	935660	-68,920	**866740**	1.137

Attachment **C**

Growth Rates

We use three different "growth rates" in this book and it is important to understand how they are calculated and the relative strengths and weaknesses of each approach.

Let's illustrate all three by considering a company's hypothetical Cash Flow from Operations (CFO) data:

	Year 6	Year 5	Year 4	Year 3	Year 2	Year 1
$ Millions	40	45	40	30	35	20
% Change:	-11.1%	12.5%	33.3%	-14.3%	75.0%	

The data shows a clear growth pattern over time, although this growth has not been steady and has experienced some volatility. This might be a typical pattern that you might see for CFO growth.

We can measure this growth in three ways:

AVERAGE GROWTH RATE (AGR):
We calculate the growth rates between the six years as shown above. We then calculate a simple average of these five figures, which equals:

$$AGR = 95.4 \div 5 = 19.1\%$$

You can immediately see a problem here. This result is much larger than either of the last two years, and in fact much greater than three of the five values. This is because we started with a low amount in year 1 and had a very big jump between years 1 and 2. This single growth value of 75% totally dominates the sum of the five numbers. This gives us an average that is unrealistically high and would be extremely difficult to sustain. Also note that this large growth rate occurred several years ago and recent growth has tapered off. AGR makes no distinction between old data and new data.

So any time that a data series shows a relatively small number followed by a relatively large number (or vice versa), that will produce a large growth number (positive or negative) that will skew the average and make it inappropriate to use in our scoring screen.

COMPOUND AVERAGE GROWTH RATE (CAGR):

This calculation considers only the first value and the last value in a series. CAGR determines the annual growth rate that would be applied to the first value and compounded over the length of the series to produce the last value.

In the case of our example, the **CAGR is 14.87%.** This rate is applied to the first value 20 and compounded five times to produce the final value 40, as follows:

Year 2:20 X 1.1487 = 22.974
Year 3:22.974 X 1.1487 = 26.390
Year 4:26.390 X 1.1487 = 30.314
Year 5:30.314 X 1.1487 = 34.822
Year 6:34.822 X 1.1487 = 40.128

Again this rate is high because we begin with a low number to start the series. As with the AGR, this rate would not be appropriate to use for scoring. In addition, all the numbers between the first and last values are irrelevant and not included in the calculation. So these interim numbers could be wildly volatile or absolutely flat – CAGR would not reflect this.

However, if any of the *interim numbers are negative*, we can still calculate CAGR. If there are *any negative numbers* in the series, we would not be able to calculate either AGR or WAGR.

WEIGHTED AVERAGE GROWTH RATE (WAGR):

Under this approach we concentrate our calculation on the most recent numbers, emphasizing the latest results over the earlier results. This seems to make logical sense in that current trends would seem to be more relevant to the future than earlier data.

Looking at the growth rates above, we would assign weights (multipliers) to each of the five growth rates, starting with a weight of 5 for the years 5-6 growth rate, and continuing down to a weight of 1 for the years 1-2 growth rate. This means that the most recent rate (5-6) will be five times more important than the earliest rate (1-2).

Years 5-6:	-11.1% X 5 =	-55.5
Years 4-5:	12.5% X 4 =	50.0
Years 3-4:	33.3% X 3 =	99.9
Years 2-3:	-14.3% X 2 =	-28.6
Years 1-2:	75.0% X 1 =	75.0
TOTAL:	15	140.8

To calculate WAGR, we divide the weighted value total (140.8) by the sum of the weights (15), so:

$$\textbf{WAGR = 140.8 / 15 = 9.38\%}$$

This is the lowest of the three calculations and in my opinion appears to be more realistic given the performance over the last three years. But it still looks a bit high to me given last year's negative growth rate. I might be tempted to throw out year 1 and calculate WAGR using only the last five years instead of the last six. In this case WAGR would be calculated as follows:

Years 5-6:	-11.1% X 4 =	-44.4%
Years 4-5:	12.5% X 3 =	37.5%
Years 3-4:	33.3% X 2 =	66.6%
Years 2-3:	-14.3% X 1 =	-14.3%
	10	45.4%

$$\textbf{WAGR = 45.4 / 10 = 4.54\%}$$

Now that number just "looks right" to me. I have no mathematics to back up that statement, but I would feel much more comfortable using that number as a screen score given the drop in year 6. There is clearly a decent growth trend here over the past six years, but the last year was a disappointment. I therefore feel that this company should be given some benefit of the doubt but I would want to be cautious in my scoring.

I generally prefer to use WAGR for two reasons. Unlike AGR, WAGR places the greatest emphasis on the most recent data. Unlike CAGR, WAGR considers all values, not just first and last. But as we have seen from the example above, you must not calculate any average with a blind eye. If there are large swings in the data, I would be careful. One single large number can skew an average in either direction. If you are not comfortable with an average, you may want to use a growth rate of zero to be conservative, or perhaps even remove the metric entirely from the screen score.

Notice that the example above relates to Cash Flow from Operations. It is here that you may find considerable volatility. But you will definitely not see such volatility when you look at dividend growth. Take a look the following dividend data:

Dividends:	2014	2013	2012	2011	2010	2009
Coca Cola	$1.22	1.12	1.02	.94	.88	.82
% Growth:	8.9%	9.8%	8.5%	6.8%	7.3%	
AGR:	8.26%					
CAGR:	8.27%					
WAGR:	8.69%					
Clorox	$2.90	2.70	2.48	2.30	2.10	1.92
% Growth:	7.4%	8.9%	7.8%	9.5%	9.4%	
AGR:	8.60%					
CAGR:	8.60%					
WAGR:	8.29%					
Microsoft	$1.21	1.07	.89	.76	.61	.52
% Growth:	13.1%	20.2%	17.1%	24.6%	17.3%	
AGR:	18.5%					
CAGR:	18.4%					
WAGR:	17.6%					

With all three stocks we see a remarkable equality between AGR and CAGR. The only difference – which is a small difference – is with WAGR. Visually you can see with each stock why WAGR is above or below the other two averages:

- Coca Cola: Recent growth rates are higher, so WAGR is higher.
- Clorox:Recent growth rates are trending down, so WAGR is lower.
- Microsoft: Last year's growth rate was significantly lower, so WAGR is clearly lower than AGR or CAGR.

So my preference remains with WAGR, although with dividends I don't think you will find a great deal of difference.

Attachment **D**

MLP Taxation: Return Of Capital

Unlike stocks that pay dividends, MLPs pay *distributions*. From a tax standpoint, there is an important difference between the two types of payments. Qualified dividend payments are taxed at long-term capital gains rates, which taxes are generally payable the year after dividend receipt. Distribution payments can create substantial multi-year tax deferrals, which result in a higher after-tax yield.

Distribution payments contain a substantial portion of Return of Capital (ROC), which represent a return of your investment – your purchase price. The ROC portion reduces your cost basis in the MLP and is not taxed until the MLP is sold, or until your cost basis is reduced to zero. So your taxes are *deferred, although not avoided*.

An example will help make this clear:

Assume: Purchase Price (Initial Cost Basis): $100.00
Annual Distribution: $ 6.00
20% classified as Current Income: $ 1.20
80% classified as Return of Capital: $ 4.80
Pre-Tax Yield: 6.0%

You would pay taxes on the current income portion, but no taxes on the ROC portion. So if your tax rate was 30%, you would pay $ .36 in taxes, netting $5.64 from the distribution. This produces an after tax yield of 5.64%. A similar dividend payment of $6.00 taxed at the long-term capital gains rate of 15% would produce a tax of $.90 and an after tax yield of 5.10%.

When this distribution is made, the MLP reduces your cost basis on its books by $4.80 to $95.20. If distributions were to continue in the same fashion going forward, your cost basis would be reduced each year by $4.80, as follows:

First year:	$95.20
Second year:	90.40
Third year:	85.60
Fourth year:	80.80
Fifth year:	76.00

Assume you sell this MLP at the end of year 5 for $100.00. You would be taxed on this amount less your cost basis, or $100.00 - $76.00 = $24.00. This represents the total ROC amount for the five year period of $4.80 X 5 = $24.00. So you have deferred payment of this tax for 5 years. Part of the tax owed at sale would be classified as long-term capital gains, and part would be considered "depreciation recapture" and taxed as ordinary income.

You can continue this deferral for years, until you sell the MLP or until your cost basis is reduced to zero. If your cost basis does reach zero, further ROC would be taxed primarily as long-term capital gains.

Attachment **E**

Interest Rate Risk

The first rule of investing in bonds, notes, preferred stocks, or other fixed income securities is this:

If interest rates rise, the value of your security will decline

If interest rates decline, the value of your security will rise

For any given change in interest rates, the amount of the change in value will depend on:

- The time remaining until maturity
- The original coupon (interest) rate

Let's look at a few examples of how this works:

Perpetual Maturity:
Preferred stock normally has no maturity date. Let's assume that the stock cannot be called or converted to common so that we have in effect a perpetual fixed income security. Assume that you invest $1000 and the coupon rate is 4.0%. You will therefore receive $40/year in perpetuity. This amount will never change.

Now assume that *interest rates rise 1%*. This means that a new investor can obtain a yield of 5% on a similar security. So this new investor would not buy your preferred stock at par ($1000) since he only receives $40 (yield of 4.0%). He would *require a discount from par* so that the fixed payment of $40/year would yield him 5%.

New Price = Old Rate / New Rate X Original Value

New Price = 4/5 X $1000
New Price = $800

So our new investor pays you $800, a reduction of 20% in value. He receives $40 per year on an investment of $800, so he achieves the new yield of 40/800 = 5%.

Now assume that *interest rates fall by 1%*. A new investor can now only obtain a yield of 3% in the market. He would be willing to *pay you a premium* for a security with a yield of 4%.

New Price = Old Rate / New Rate X Original Value

New Price = 4/3 X $1000
New Price = $1333.33

The new investor pays you $1333.33, an increase of 33.3% in value. He receives $40 per year on an investment of $1333.33, a yield of 3%.

So looking at a perpetual maturity, a change in interest rates has the maximum impact on your value today, as the change affects investor return over the longest period (infinity) possible.

Non–Perpetual Maturity:
Let's take the same example, only assume now that we are considering a note that matures in five years.

The annual payments to be received on this note are as follows:

Total payments = $40 + $40 + $40 + $40 + $1040 = $1200.
This cash flow stream has a *Net Present Value of $1000 using an earnings rate of 4.0%.*

But now assume that interest rates rise by 1%. A new investor would expect an *earnings rate of 5%*.

So using the same cash flow stream but increasing the discount *rate to 5%, we get a NPV of $956.71.*

This is what the new investor would pay for this security, which represents a loss of $43.29, or 4.33%.

So with an increase of 1% in interest rates, our loss was 20% with a perpetual maturity, but only 4.3% with a five-year maturity.

Using the same example of a 4% coupon rate, below is a table that shows the drop in principal value when interest rates rise 1%, assuming different maturities:

4% Coupon Rate 1% Rise in Interest Rates		
Maturity	Value of a $1000 Note	% Loss of Principal
1 Year	$ 990.48	0.95%
3 Years	$ 972.77	2.72%
5 Years	$ 956.71	4.33%
7 Years	$ 942.14	5.79%
10 Years	$ 922.78	7.72%
15 Years	$ 896.20	10.38%
Perpetual	$ 800.00	20.00%

Given a change in interest rates, the change in principal value depends <u>first</u> on the years to maturity.

The longer the years to maturity, the greater the change in principal value.

Looking at this example, it appears that the percentage change in principal is just slightly less than the number of years to maturity. Since the duration of a bond is generally slightly less than the years to maturity, a general rule followed by bond investors is:

For a one percent change in interest rates, the percentage change in principal value will approximately equal the duration of the bond.

The other factor that will determine the change in principal for a given change in interest rates is the coupon rate of the bond itself. Let's rearrange the table above to now assume a constant maturity (let us say five years) and a differing level of coupon rates:

Five Year Maturity 1% Rise in Interest Rates		
Coupon Rate	Value of a $1000 Note	% Loss of Principal
1.0%	$ 952.87	4.71%
3.0%	$ 955.48	4.45%
5.0%	$957.88	4.21%
7.0%	$960.07	3.99%
10.0%	$963.04	3.69%
12.0%	$964.83	3.52%

Given a change in interest rates, the change in principal value depends secondly on the coupon rate.

While the effect is not as pronounced as the years to maturity,

The higher the coupon rate (IE: High Yield Bonds), the smaller the change in principal value.

Attachment **F**

Adjustment: Real Estate Investment Trusts

The net income earned by any company is calculated after a deduction for depreciation expense, in which the value of fixed assets (buildings and equipment) is reduced on the balance sheet. This expense represents an approximation of the "wear and tear" deterioration that applies gradually over time to any fixed asset. This is simply an accounting adjustment that does not involve any actual outlay of cash.

In the case of REITs, depreciation is a major expense relative to net income, and therefore REIT net income seriously understates the true cash flow generated that is available to pay dividends. So net income (earnings) per share is not a good metric to use in evaluating REIT dividend protection.

Instead of calculating the ratio of dividends paid / earnings per share, we look at another metric to measure REIT dividend coverage. This metric is "Funds From Operations" (FFO). This figure is determined by adding depreciation to net income, and excluding gains or losses on the sale of property.

Unfortunately, this figure is not generally found on websites and it is necessary to go to the company's regulatory filings to find it. It is usually found under the section "Management's Discussion and Analysis." (Morningstar provides access to such reports under the "Filings" tab). Note that if preferred dividends are paid, you want the FFO figure applicable to common shares (after preferred payments).

A refinement to FFO is "Adjusted Funds From Operations" (AFFO). AFFO begins with the FFO calculation but makes a deduction for the expenses incurred to maintain existing properties. However, there is no consensus as to the precise definition of AFFO, which varies from REIT to REIT. Some REITS calculate this number and include it in their regulatory filings; others do not. So I use FFO to measure the Dividend Payout Ratio since it is always available and consistently defined.

Therefore, when using the model to evaluate a REIT, the Dividend Payout Ratio is calculated as follows:

3 Year Weighted Average Ratio: Dividends ÷ FFO

You will find that this ratio is higher than the dividend coverage ratio of most non-REIT corporations. This is not surprising given the requirement that REITS pay very high dividends. *Therefore, in Preliminary REIT Screens, I increase my maximum payout ratio from .75 to .90. However, my Final Screen weighting and multiplier remain the same.*

This is the only change I make to the model. All other metrics, weights, and multipliers remain the same.

Attachment **G**

Adjustment: Master Limited Partnerships

Master Limited Partnerships are similar to REITs in that they are both capital intensive entities that invest heavily in fixed assets. Hence depreciation expense is significant for both, and net income (earnings) is not a good metric to measure dividend/distribution coverage.

The metric used to evaluate MLP distribution coverage is "Distributable Cash Flow" (DCF). This metric is calculated as follows:

Net Income:
PLUS: Depreciation and Amortization Expense
Loss on sale/retirement of assets (asset impairment charges)
LESS: Gain on sale/retirement of assets
Maintenance (sustaining) capital expense

Adjustments are also made for derivative gains/losses, inventory adjustments, deferred income tax expense/benefit, and acquisition/ restructuring charges.

Again, the DCF number is not found on any website and you will have to go to the company's regulatory filings to find this number under "Management Discussion and Analysis" or under "Selected Financial Data." Morningstar provides access to these reports under the "filings" tab.

Regarding distributions, it is important to include *all* distributions, including distributions to limited unit holders, general partners, and non-related entities. Total distributions are itemized in the "Consolidated Statements of Cash Flows" found in the company's audited financial statements.

Therefore, MLP distribution coverage is calculated as follows:

3 Year Weighted Average Ratio: Total Distributions / DCF

As with REITs, this ratio is high given that virtually all available cash, excluding certain reserves, is distributed monthly or quarterly. I increase my maximum payout ratio from .75 to .95 in the Preliminary screen, but leave all other weightings the same in the Final Screen.

Attachment **H**

Cash Flow Coverage Of Dividends

The Dividend Payout Ratio is defined in this book as Dividends per share ÷ Earnings per share. This is the standard metric for measuring the "safety" of the dividend. The ratio is easy to understand and easy to calculate. The majority of investors use this ratio in analyzing dividend coverage, as earnings are broadly perceived to be the ultimate source of dividend payments. I think this ratio is a good one to use when you first start out as a "do it yourself" investor.

That said, the fact remains that *dividends are actually paid from cash flow, not from earnings.* I don't want to get sidetracked into a long discussion on accounting, but I think it is important to get a basic understanding as to the difference between the two terms.

Earnings (Net Income) are calculated according to the schedule set forth in a company's Income Statement. The Income Statement is one of the three primary financial statements that a company issues to show its overall financial condition. The statement looks like this:

Gross Sales
    Less: Cost of Goods Sold (Labor, Materials, Depreciation)
= Gross Profit
    Less: Selling and Administrative Costs
= Net Operating Income
    Less: Interest Expense
= Net Income Before Taxes
    Less: Taxes
= Net Income (Earnings)

This statement reflects "the bottom line" in that it shows what company operations added to the Net Worth of the business. *However, Net Income is only a part of the cash flow generated by operations (CFO).* What are the differences between the two terms?

- *Net Income contains certain charges/costs that do not involve actual outlays of cash.*

Usually the largest such cost is depreciation. The company recognizes that all fixed assets have a certain useful life, and it makes a periodic charge against fixed assets to reduce their book value. But this charge is strictly a bookkeeping entry. The value of the asset is written down, and the amount of income earned is written down an equal amount. But no cash is involved. *So Net Income understates Cash Flow from Operations (CFO) through such non-cash charges.*

- *Net Income tells us nothing about changes in the company's working capital accounts.*

Working Capital includes all of a company's Current Assets, less all Current liabilities. Current Assets include cash and items that should quickly convert to cash, such as Accounts Receivable and Inventory. Current Liabilities include all items due for payment within a year, such as Accounts Payable, Accruals, and short-term Debt.

All of these short-term assets and liabilities are constantly changing as the company manufactures and sells its products or services. If the company is growing, it is likely that it will need more inventory and have to carry a higher level of accounts receivable. *This consumes cash.* On the other hand, accounts payable may increase as the company buys more inventory, short-term bank loans may increase, and accrued expenses may grow with higher payroll and taxes. *This supplies cash.* All of these changes have to be considered to determine the full effect that operations have on the company's cash position.

Therefore, the company will prepare a *Statement of Cash Flows from Operations.* This is the second financial statement that reflects the financial condition of the firm. To simplify this statement down to its basics, it will be formatted as follows:

> Net Income
> > Plus: Depreciation and other non-cash expenses
> > Plus/Minus Net Change in Working Capital
> = Cash Flow from Operations (CFO)

A significant number of investors point out that it is CFO that reflects the real source of dividend payments – and dividend protection – as CFO shows what cash is actually available to pay out. But before they calculate dividend coverage, these investors also want to consider another major cash outlay – capital expenses for fixed assets. *They focus on "Free Cash Flow" – Cash Flow from Operations(CFO) less Capital Expenses (CAPEX) – as the proper metric to calculate dividend coverage.*

Therefore for these investors the calculation of dividend coverage is not based on earnings, but is calculated as:

Free Cash Flow (FCF) = Cash Flow from Operations (CFO) – Capital Expenditures (CAPEX)

Payout Ratio = Dividends ÷ Free Cash Flow

This is a very conservative approach to dividend coverage. *The implication is that the company should be self-funding.* The company should be able to: 1) Fund all net increases to working capital, 2) Fund all capital expenditures, and 3) Fund all dividends – and still have a healthy remainder left over to provide good dividend coverage. *The company should not have to borrow at all,* except for short-term (self-liquidating) working capital support, or perhaps to fund a major expansion or acquisition.

While I like the logic of this approach, it is often hard for capital intensive companies such as utilities, telecoms, and energy to pass this test. It is virtually impossible to pass this test if such a company is expanding or involved in heavy retrofitting. And so I find that some authors fall back on an earnings formula to measure dividend coverage for these industries. But that doesn't satisfy me, because then you are using two different standards to measure dividend coverage.

I wrestled with this issue and ultimately decided to adopt an approach to measure dividend coverage which is similar to the approach used in Master Limited Partnerships. I decided that a company should *generate enough cash flow to pay for maintenance capital expenses.* This seems reasonable to me because this is another cost of keeping the business functioning as it stands – without expansion. If the company wants to expand its fixed asset base, that is another decision that may require external financing. So my formula for dividend coverage is:

Payout Ratio = Dividends ÷ CFO – Maintenance Capital Expenses

The issue now is that C corporations do not usually publish their maintenance expenses. *So I use depreciation expense as a proxy for maintenance expense.* Depreciation expense represents the estimated annual deterioration of fixed assets, and while there is no immediate connection between this number and actual maintenance expense, I feel that over time there should be a close connection between depreciation and maintenance. At the very least, they both share the same conceptual framework – the cost of replacing fixed assets as they wear out.

I make one adjustment to the depreciation amount. Since depreciation is based on an asset's original cost, I think that current replacement cost would be higher, so I gross up the depreciation expense by 15%. Therefore the ratio that *I now use for all C corporations to measure dividend coverage is*:

Dividend Payout Ratio = Dividends ÷ Cash Flow from Operations – (1.15) (Depreciation)

It can still be a stretch for capital intensive companies to score well with this ratio, but I think this is a fair standard that all companies should meet, and now I have one single ratio to apply universally to all corporations.

Attachment **I**

"Get 5 in 5" Rule

After finishing the book I had a thought about dividend growth that seemed to make sense to me, and which also led me to create a catchy phrase: "Get 5 in 5." What that means is that you *set a goal to achieve a minimum 5.0% yield on cost for any security by the end of five years.*

In order to do that, the table below shows various initial yields on cost, and presents the compound growth rates you would need in order to achieve a 5% yield within 5 years:

Initial Yield On Cost (YOC)	Compound Growth Rate	Five Year YOC
2.50%	14.9%	5.0%
2.75%	12.7%	5.0%
3.00%	10.7%	5.0%
3.25%	9.0%	5.0%
3.50%	7.4%	5.0%
3.75%	5.9%	5.0%
4.00%	4.6%	5.0%
4.25%	3.3%	5.0%
4.50%	2.1%	5.0%

I think this is a fairly aggressive goal and I would admit that there are several securities in my portfolio that fall short of this goal. However, every security I own but one is projected to achieve a 5-year YOC of 4.5% or higher. So if 5.0% is a bit of a stretch, I would definitely recommend a minimum fall back goal of 4.5%. For those near to or into retirement, I think that the 5.0% rule should be a pretty firm requirement.

Selected Reading List

Josh Peters CFA, *The Ultimate Dividend Playbook*, Hoboken NJ: John Wiley & Sons, 2008
> This is The Bible. If you are only going to read one book on dividend investing, *this is the one.*

Benjamin Graham, *The Intelligent Investor – Revised Edition*, New York: HarperCollins, 1973, 2003

Jeremy J. Siegel, *Stocks for the Long Run*, New York: McGraw Hill, 2014

Kelley Wright, *Dividends Still Don't Lie*, Hoboken NJ: John Wiley & Sons, 2010

Mark T. Hebner, *Index Funds*, Irvine CA: IFA Publishing, 2011

Bruce C. Miller CFP, *Retirement Investing for Income Only*, Middletown DE: 2014

Lawrence Carrel, *Dividend Stocks for Dummies*, New York: Wiley Publishing, 2010

68397665R10160

Made in the USA
Charleston, SC
11 March 2017